John Montana came to First Baptist Church in Danville to hear his brother sing during the Easter service. A drug addict and biker, hearing his brother sing was all he committed himself to that day.

Until he decided to follow the Lord.

"I ended up getting up and walking the aisle and giving my life to Jesus that day," he said. "I got up and told the church I was a low life, no-good-for-nothing piece of cr**. I was crying and I was tired, you know. I was tired of the stupidness, the ignorance I lived in."

A week later, he was leading the Celebrate Recovery support group for the church. He stopped using drugs. He became a better husband. He started riding with the local Bikers for Christ chapter, where he has led numerous people to Christ.

God began radically changing his life that Easter, a process that continues today.

"God's replenishing this whole life of mine. … I started with [this wayward lifestyle]," he said. "My son's finishing with it. My daughter's already back in church now. It's just going to become a big Christian family that's going to have one big ministry after another going into these prisons, into the juvenile detention centers talking to these kids."

Montana's story is echoed by many in the congregation that started with 17 people as well as the help of Texas Baptists and the Texas Baptist Cooperative Program several years ago. Many of the more than 100 people who attend each week have pasts that include combinations of incarceration, substance abuse, homelessness and physical abuse.

Church members use their backgrounds to help them minister in prisons. They care for the homeless. They look for ways to help those in need.

The congregation is a place where people can encounter God no matter their past, said Pastor Freeman Pierce, who faced his own struggles with alcohol abuse before being saved, kicking off 41 years of sobriety.

"We really don't care where they've been or what they've done," Pierce said. "We want to know where they are and where they want to get to."

Pierce first encountered Ross and Kimberly Brown at a homeless ministry. At the time, they were struggling with drug and alcohol abuse.

"We were homeless," Kimberly said. "We were sleeping in the woods. We had nowhere to go."

Pierce brought them to a nearby fast food restaurant where he shared the "foundational life principle" with them out of 1 Corinthians

– a relationship with Christ should guide a person's life. The couple made professions of faith over hamburgers that afternoon.

Pierce found the couple a place to stay. They got clean. Ross dealt with a legal issue. The congregation rallied around the young people. Now they are both clean, have their own home and twins on the way.

Ross sees the difference between how First Baptist Church views him and how others do.

"People look at me on the streets with all these tattoos and they frown on it," Ross said. "[The church members] open their arms to me."

Pierce met Westleigh Boatman roughly five years ago in prison. Though he was initially reluctant to visit with Pierce, Boatman soon began taking the pastor's words about the gospel to heart. He accepted Christ while behind bars and continued growing in his faith with the help of Pierce. When Boatman was released, Pierce was there to pick him up.

"Since I came out, I've had contact with my parents, I've been in Celebrate Recovery, I work at the church, I sing in the choir," Boatman said with a smile. "I enjoy being here. I love everybody who's here. I've lived with the pastor. I've got a job."

The church's generosity has been overwhelming for Boatman to the point that his life changed dramatically.

"Everything left and right has been given to me. It's all by the grace of God that I've got it," he said. "Without Him, I'd be out on the street or back in jail by now. Who I am now is not who I was five years ago. I'm a Christian. **I'm a saved man."**

GET THE MISSION

DO MORE GOOD FOR MORE PEOPLE.

"CP" (Cooperative Program) is a Missions Co-op that lets people like you work together to do more of God's work.

House more orphans.   Feed & clothe more needy people.   Care for more sick people.

Reach more prisoners.   Start more churches.   Fund more missionaries.   Help more people in disasters.

Share the hope of Christ with more people.

IT ALL STARTS WITH YOU.

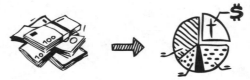

You get paid for your job, and you give some money to your church to do God's work.

Your church uses the money for missions and ministries. But since even a large church has limits...

...it has a larger missions partner, a state convention – the BGCT – that has connections worldwide.
So your church and others across Texas give via "CP," and we do far more together than any church can do alone.

"CP" HELPS YOU AND YOUR CHURCH
SHARE THE GIFTS GOD HAS GIVEN YOU.

Share money, brains & talent. "CP" reduces duplication of effort, checks worthy causes,
makes funds work harder. "CP" coordinates mission trips, volunteer efforts, etc.

Share prayers. "CP" unites the spiritual power of 2 million Texas Baptists.

Learn more about all you support through "CP" at texasbaptists.org/cp.

TO ASK QUESTIONS OR GET MORE INVOLVED, CALL 888-244-9400.

TEXAS ★ BAPTISTS
BAPTIST GENERAL CONVENTION OF TEXAS

333 N. Washington | Dallas, TX 75246-1798 | 888.244.9400 | www.texasbaptists.org

BaptistWay Adult Bible Study Guide®

The Gospel of Mark
People Responding to Jesus

BOB DeFOOR
BOB DUNCAN
CHARLES GLIDEWELL
TOM HOWE
GARY LONG

BAPTISTWAYPRESS®
Dallas, Texas

The Gospel of Mark: People Responding to Jesus—BaptistWay Adult Bible Study Guide®

BAPTISTWAY PRESS® Leadership Team
Executive Director, Baptist General Convention of Texas: David Hardage
Director, Education/Discipleship Center: Chris Liebrum
Director, Bible Study/Discipleship Team: Phil Miller
Publisher, BaptistWay Press®: Scott Stevens

Publishing consultant and editor: Ross West
Cover and Interior Design and Production: Desktop Miracles, Inc.
Printing: Data Reproductions Corporation

First edition: December 2012
ISBN–13: 978–1–931060–00–4

How to Make the Best Use of This Issue

Whether you're the teacher or a student—

1. Start early in the week before your class meets.

2. Overview the study. Review the table of contents and read the study introduction. Try to see how each lesson relates to the overall study.

3. Use your Bible to read and consider prayerfully the Scripture passages for the lesson. (You'll see that each writer has chosen a favorite translation for the lessons in this issue. You're free to use the Bible translation you prefer and compare it with the translation chosen for that unit, of course.)

4. After reading all the Scripture passages in your Bible, then read the writer's comments. The comments are intended to be an aid to your study of the Bible.

5. Read the small articles—"sidebars"—in each lesson. They are intended to provide additional, enrichment information and inspiration and to encourage thought and application.

6. Try to answer for yourself the questions included in each lesson. They're intended to encourage further thought and application, and they can also be used in the class session itself.

If you're the teacher—

A. Do all of the things just mentioned, of course. As you begin the study with your class, be sure to find a way to help your class know the date on which each lesson will be studied. You might do this in one or more of the following ways:

    *   In the first session of the study, briefly overview the study by identifying with your class the date on which each lesson will be studied. Lead your class to write the date in the table of contents on page 9 and on the first page of each lesson.

- Make and post a chart that indicates the date on which each lesson will be studied.
- If all of your class has e-mail, send them an e-mail with the dates the lessons will be studied.
- Provide a bookmark with the lesson dates. You may want to include information about your church and then use the bookmark as an outreach tool, too. A model for a bookmark can be downloaded from www.baptistwaypress.org on the Resources for Adults page.
- Develop a sticker with the lesson dates, and place it on the table of contents or on the back cover.

B. Get a copy of the *Teaching Guide,* a companion piece to this *Study Guide.* The *Teaching Guide* contains additional Bible comments plus two teaching plans. The teaching plans in the *Teaching Guide* are intended to provide practical, easy-to-use teaching suggestions that will work in your class.

C. After you've studied the Bible passage, the lesson comments, and other material, use the teaching suggestions in the *Teaching Guide* to help you develop your plan for leading your class in studying each lesson.

D. Teaching resource items for use as handouts are available free at www.baptistwaypress.org.

E. You may want to get the additional adult Bible study comments— *Adult Online Bible Commentary*—by Dr. Jim Denison (president, Denison Forum on Truth and Culture, and theologian-in-residence, Baptist General Convention of Texas). Call 1–866–249–1799 or e-mail baptistway@texasbaptists.org to order *Adult Online Bible Commentary.* It is available only in electronic format (PDF) from our website, www.baptistwaypress.org. The price of these comments for the entire study is $6 for individuals and $25 for a group of five. A church or class that participates in our advance order program for free shipping can receive *Adult Online Bible Commentary* free. Call 1–866–249–1799 or see www.baptistwaypress.org to purchase or for information on participating in our free shipping program for the next study.

F. Additional teaching plans are also available in electronic format (PDF) by calling 1–866–249–1799. The price of these additional teaching plans for the entire study is $5 for an individual and $20 for a group of five. A church or class that participates in our advance order program for free shipping can receive *Adult Online Teaching Plans* free. Call 1–866–249–1799 or see www.baptistwaypress.org for information on participating in our free shipping program for the next study.

G. You also may want to get the enrichment teaching help that is provided on the internet by the *Baptist Standard* at www.baptiststandard.com. (Other class participants may find this information helpful, too.) Call 214–630–4571 to begin your subscription to the printed or electronic edition of the *Baptist Standard.*

H. Enjoy leading your class in discovering the meaning of the Scripture passages and in applying these passages to their lives.

DO YOU USE A KINDLE?

This BaptistWay *Adult Bible Study Guide* plus *Living Generously for Jesus' Sake; Profiles in Character; Amos, Hosea, Isaiah, Micah; The Gospel of Matthew; The Gospel of John: Part One; The Gospel of John: Part Two; The Book of Acts: Time to Act on Acts 1:8;* and *The Corinthian Letters: Imperatives for an Imperfect Church* are now available in a Kindle edition. The easiest way to find these materials is to search for "BaptistWay" on your Kindle or go to www.amazon.com/kindle and do a search for "BaptistWay." The Kindle edition can be studied not only on a Kindle but also on a PC, Mac, iPhone, iPad, Blackberry, or Android phone using the Kindle app available free from amazon.com/kindle.

AUDIO BIBLE STUDY LESSONS

Do you want to use your walk/run/ride, etc. time to study the Bible? Or maybe you're a college student who wants to listen to the lesson on your iPod®? Or maybe you're looking for a way to study the Bible when you just can't find time to read? Or maybe you know someone who has difficulty seeing to read even our *Large Print Study Guide*?

Then try our audio Bible study lessons, available on this study plus *Living Generously for Jesus' Sake; Profiles in Character; Amos, Hosea, Isaiah, Micah; The Gospel of Matthew; The Gospel of Luke; The Gospel of John: Part One; The Gospel of John: Part Two; The Book of Acts; The Corinthian Letters; Galatians and 1 & 2 Thessalonians;* and *The Letters of James and John.* For more information or to order, call 1–866–249–1799 or e-mail baptistway@texasbaptists.org. The files are downloaded from our website. You'll need an audio player that plays MP3 files (like an iPod®, but many MP3 players are available), or you can listen on a computer.

Writers of This Study Guide

Tom Howe, who wrote lessons one through three, is the senior pastor of Birdville Baptist Church, Haltom City, Texas. Dr. Howe is a graduate of East Texas Baptist University (B.S.), Beeson Divinity School at Samford University (M. Div.), and Southwestern Baptist Theological Seminary (D. Min.).

Bob DeFoor of Harrodsburg, Kentucky, wrote lessons four through six. Dr. DeFoor served more than forty years as pastor of churches in Kentucky and Georgia, serving the last twenty-eight prior to retirement as pastor of Harrodsburg Baptist Church. Both Bob and his wife Sandy are native Georgians, and both are graduates of Baylor University, Waco, Texas.

Gary Long wrote lessons seven through nine in the *Adult Bible Study Guide* and also "Teaching Plans" for lessons seven through nine in the *Adult Bible Teaching Guide*. Gary serves First Baptist Church, Gaithersburg, Maryland, as pastor, and formerly served Willow Meadows Baptist Church, Houston, Texas. He has also served churches in North Carolina and Virginia.

Bob Duncan, writer of lessons ten and eleven, served as pastor in three churches in Texas and Arkansas prior to a thirty-two year career as chaplain with Baylor Health Care System in Dallas, Texas, from which he recently retired. Dr. Duncan and his wife, Donna, are members of South Garland Baptist Church in Garland, Texas. Bob is a graduate of Ouachita Baptist University in Arkadelphia, Arkansas, and holds the Doctor of Theology degree from Southwestern Baptist Theological Seminary in Fort Worth, Texas.

Charles Glidewell wrote lessons twelve, thirteen, and the Christmas lesson in the *Adult Bible Study Guide* as well as "Teaching Plans" for these lessons in the *Adult Bible Teaching Guide.* He is the senior pastor of First Baptist Church, New London, New Hampshire. He received the Master of Divinity degree from Logsdon Seminary, Abilene, Texas.

The Gospel of Mark: People Responding to Jesus

Introducing

THE GOSPEL OF MARK:
People Responding to Jesus

Approaching This Study of the Gospel of Mark

From the very first verse of the Gospel of Mark, we know what Mark thinks of Jesus and, indeed, what Mark wants *us* to think of Jesus. Jesus is "Christ, the Son of God," and Jesus brings and is "good news." The rest of the Gospel of Mark amplifies these truths. The Gospel of Mark shows us in Jesus' words and deeds, with an emphasis in Mark's Gospel on the deeds, who Jesus truly is.

There's more. The Gospel of Mark lets us see who Jesus is by letting us look at him through others' eyes—the eyes of the people in Jesus' life. That aspect of the Gospel of Mark is the framework for this study.

A number of people in the Gospel of Mark are shown responding to Jesus, in both positive and negative ways. We will seek to learn from the Gospel of Mark about who Jesus is and how we need to respond to him ourselves by studying Scripture passages on these people's responses to Jesus.

The thirteen lessons of this study of the Gospel of Mark focus on "People Responding to Jesus." As we look at their responses, our goal will be to receive "the good news of Jesus Christ, the Son of God" (Mark 1:1) and respond positively to that "good news."

Since the beginning of our BaptistWay Bible study series, we have focused on the Gospel of Mark twice previously. (This particular study appears in our thirteenth year of publishing. The latest previous study was five years earlier.) The first study is titled *Jesus in the Gospel of Mark*. The second study is titled *The Gospel of Mark: Jesus' Words and Words*. Both of these studies are still in print as well as being available in PDF format. Each of these studies—this one as well as the previous two—is different from the others in its approach in the individual lessons.[1] None of these studies are just repeats of the previous one, and that's the situation with this study as well.

We think studying Scriptures directly about Jesus on a regular basis is important, and so we provide a study of a Gospel each year. Each study is different, however, although we obviously over a period of years will study a Gospel more than once.

A Little Background to the Gospel of Mark

The Gospel of Mark likely is the first written Gospel, probably appearing some thirty-five or so years after Jesus' death and resurrection. The early Christian preachers had preached the gospel, and now Mark wrote down the message that had been proclaimed about Jesus through the decades. In fact, the Gospel of Mark may well reflect Peter's preaching, as many Bible commentators suggest.

Mark's first readers might have been facing persecution in Rome during the middle of the 60s. In such a situation, a decision had to be made about Jesus. Christians needed to know what kind of person and message could demand their devotion even to the point of calling for their lives. Prospective Christians needed this information, too, as they pondered whether committing their lives to Jesus was worth it. Moreover, as the eyewitnesses to Jesus' earthly life began to pass away, these early Christians also needed information they could share with others and so lead them to commitment to Jesus.

Responding to Jesus in Our Day

The question about how to respond to Jesus continues to face people in our own day. Who is Jesus, and how shall *we* respond to him? In sixteen swiftly-moving chapters, the Gospel of Mark tells the story of Jesus in a way that calls for a decision by every person. Mark's message about Jesus also provides hope and assurance that commitment—the kind of commitment that means taking up our own cross and following him—is indeed worthwhile.

We learn much about life, including about the Christian faith, through other people. Let the people in the Gospel of Mark on which these lessons are based help you learn about Jesus and respond to him in full commitment.

Note: Since the time of the first release of these materials includes the Christmas holiday, a Christmas lesson is included to meet the needs of churches who wish to have an emphasis on Christmas at this time.[2]

THE GOSPEL OF MARK: PEOPLE RESPONDING TO JESUS

Lesson 1	John the Baptist: Preparing for Jesus	Mark 1:1–11
Lesson 2	Peter: Telling Jesus He's Wrong	Mark 1:16–18; 8:27–33; 14:26–31, 66–72; 16:5–7
Lesson 3	James and John: We Are First	Mark 1:19–20; 3:13–17; 10:35–45
Lesson 4	Levi: Outsiders Welcome	Mark 2:13–17
Lesson 5	A Disturbed Man: Freed from Being Out of Control	Mark 5:1–20
Lesson 6	Two Desperate People: Relying On Jesus	Mark 5:22–43
Lesson 7	Hometown People: Stuck in the Ordinary	Mark 6:1–6
Lesson 8	The Religious Leaders: Bound By Tradition	Mark 7:1–23
Lesson 9	The Disciples: Slow to Get It	Mark 6:45–52; 8:1–21
Lesson 10	The Law Expert: Asking About What Matters Most	Mark 12:28–34
Lesson 11	The Woman at Bethany: Honoring Jesus Extravagantly	Mark 14:1–9
Lesson 12	Judas: Doing the Unthinkable	Mark 14:10–11, 17–21, 41–50
Lesson 13	Women at the Cross and the Tomb: Serving Jesus to the End	Mark 15:40—16:8

Additional Resources for Studying the Gospel of Mark:[3]

William Barclay. *The Gospel of Mark*. Revised edition. Philadelphia: The Westminster Press, 1975.

James A. Brooks. *Mark*. The New American Commentary. Volume 23. Nashville, Tennessee: Broadman Press, 1991.

Sharyn Dowd. *Reading Mark: A Literary and Theological Commentary on the Second Gospel*. Reading the New Testament Series. Macon, Georgia: Smyth and Helwys Publishing, 2000.

David E. Garland. *Mark*. The NIV Application Commentary. Grand Rapids, Michigan: Zondervan Publishing House, 1996.

Craig S. Keener. *IVP Bible Background Commentary: New Testament*. Downers Grove, Illinois: InterVarsity Press, 1993.

William L. Lane. *The Gospel According to Mark*. The New International Commentary on the New Testament. Grand Rapids, Michigan: William B. Eerdmans Publishing Company, 1974.

Lloyd J. Ogilvie. *Life Without Limits*: Waco, Texas: Word Books, Publisher, 1975.

Pheme Perkins. "Mark." *The New Interpreter's Bible*, Volume VIII. Nashville, Tennessee: Abingdon Press, 1995.

A. T. Robertson. *Word Pictures in the New Testament*. Volume I. Nashville, Tennessee: Broadman Press, 1930.

NOTES

1. See www.baptistwaypress.org.

2. Unless otherwise indicated, all Scripture quotations on the back cover, in "Introducing The Gospel of Mark: People Responding to Jesus," in lessons 7—9, 12–13, and in the Christmas lesson are taken from the New Revised Standard Version Bible.

3. Listing a book does not imply full agreement by the writers or BAPTISTWAY with all of its comments.

John the Baptist: Preparing for Jesus

FOCAL TEXT
Mark 1:1–11

BACKGROUND
Mark 1:1–15; 6:14–29; 11:27–33

MAIN IDEA
John the Baptist proclaimed the message of preparing for Jesus' coming by repenting of sin, seeking God's forgiveness.

QUESTION TO EXPLORE
In what ways do we need to prepare the way for Jesus?

STUDY AIM
To describe how John the Baptist prepared the way for Jesus and to identify how I will prepare his way today

QUICK READ
John the Baptist prepared his world for Jesus. Are we doing the same for our world?

The Beginning of the Gospel (1:1)

Mark 1:1 is actually the title of the book and not just the first verse. The title sets four themes of Mark's writing: (1) the gospel; (2) Jesus is the Christ; (3) Jesus is the Son of God; and (4) this is only the beginning. Consider each of these themes.

(1) "Gospel" means *good news*. The salvation that Jesus provides for all who believe is indeed good news. Mark may have been the first New Testament book written; Mark was almost certainly the first to write a gospel. Imagine Mark's first readers reading the first Scripture written in more than 400 years and the book starts with this refreshing thought: *here is the gospel—the good news.* Now realize that for many people today who have not heard the complete gospel story, the good news is still just as much good news as it ever was.

(2) *Christ* is from a Greek word that means *the Anointed One*. The Hebrew equivalent is *Messiah*. The Old Testament contains the message that the Messiah would be the one to come and bring the conclusion of God's work on earth. Although Mark's readers knew the first verse declared that Jesus is the Christ, they would see as they read the Gospel of Mark that Jesus allowed each person to discover who he is on his or her own. It was not until late in Jesus' ministry that any of his disciples dared to declare Jesus the Christ. (Peter finally said it in Mark 8:29.) The Jewish leaders were ready to convict Jesus when he answered "I am" to their inquiry, "Are you the Christ?" (Mark 14:61–62). Likewise, we each must come to the conclusion about whether Jesus is Christ.

(3) In the first verse, Mark also set out to establish that Jesus is "the Son of God." Mark also was careful in using this title throughout his Gospel as he was with the title "Christ." Mark wrote that Jesus was called "Son of God" six times (including variations), only once by another human, and that at the end of the Gospel, by the Roman centurion at the death of Jesus (Mark 15:39). The Father uttered it at Jesus' baptism (1:11) and at Jesus' transfiguration (9:7). Demons declared it twice (3:11; 5:7). Jesus himself affirmed it when his accusers asked him at his trial before the high priest (14:61–62).[1]

(4) Mark wrote "the beginning of the gospel of Jesus . . ." within the title of the book, which has become the first verse. He was not referring to the first days of the ministry of Jesus. Mark was calling his entire book "the beginning." His implication was that the gospel continues on

and on after the Book of Mark closes. The point is still true today for each person who receives the gospel; the story continues beyond the initial steps of faith.[2]

MARK 1:1–11

[1] The beginning of the gospel about Jesus Christ, the Son of God.

[2] It is written in Isaiah the prophet:

"I will send my messenger ahead of you, who will prepare your way"—

[3] "a voice of one calling in the desert, 'Prepare the way for the Lord, make straight paths for him.'"

[4] And so John came, baptizing in the desert region and preaching a baptism of repentance for the forgiveness of sins. [5] The whole Judean countryside and all the people of Jerusalem went out to him. Confessing their sins, they were baptized by him in the Jordan River. [6] John wore clothing made of camel's hair, with a leather belt around his waist, and he ate locusts and wild honey. [7] And this was his message: "After me will come one more powerful than I, the thongs of whose sandals I am not worthy to stoop down and untie. [8] I baptize you with water, but he will baptize you with the Holy Spirit."

[9] At that time Jesus came from Nazareth in Galilee and was baptized by John in the Jordan. [10] As Jesus was coming up out of the water, he saw heaven being torn open and the Spirit descending on him like a dove. [11] And a voice came from heaven: "You are my Son, whom I love; with you I am well pleased."

Preparing for Jesus in the Wilderness (1:2–3)

Mark quoted in verses 2–3 a combination of Exodus 23:20, Malachi 3:1, and Isaiah 40:3, although he cited only Isaiah. This seems inappropriate in our modern approach, but it was the norm in Mark's day. He listed the greatest source and the one that tied together the others—Isaiah. The more significant point is that Mark was immediately drawing on

Scripture to establish the grounds for his Gospel. The New Testament is not a repudiation of the Old but a smooth continuation of it. Believers today also need to find the foundation of faith in Scripture, not in personal experience, pop culture, or contemporary morality.

The story of John the Baptist is known so well that it seems natural, but in reality it would have been odd for John to begin preaching in the wilderness. The masses were in Jerusalem, especially the religious crowd. Why did John go to the desert to preach? The answer is found in the clue that Mark provides by quoting Isaiah 40. The first thirty-nine chapters of Isaiah deal with the judgment of God; chapter 40 marks a transition point. From that point on, Isaiah wrote about comforting the people of God, delivering them, saving them, and bringing them back to himself (with the Suffering Servant). Although the wilderness mentioned in Isaiah 40 can refer to a physical desert, it certainly also represents a spiritual wilderness in which the people of God are lost (as in the days of Moses). John's preaching in the wilderness also was directed at a people lost in a spiritual wasteland. John the Baptist did not focus on the people who thought they had all the religious answers but on the people who were broken and lost. Jesus continued the same ministry.

If John and Jesus were so interested in those in the wilderness and if they intentionally avoided the religious leaders (the Pharisees, Sadducees, Herodians, Essenes, scribes, and so forth), what should be the focus of

FORGIVENESS

You cannot receive forgiveness from God without confession and repentance. There is no place in Scripture that God voluntarily forgives someone without that person first asking for it, and yet many Christians seem to live as though they assume God is happy enough with them and will forgive them just because. God will not honor such a Christian life.

There are usually three types of sins that we need to turn over to the Lord: (1) those we know about but have not confessed; (2) those we have confessed but have not repented of—changed our behavior; and (3) those we do not know about. We need to discover whatever unknown sin in our lives is hindering God's blessing. We then must confess the sin God reveals in us and repent of it by changing our behavior.

true ministry today? It seems that many Christian leaders are interested in reaching the same pool of the religious to the exclusion of those who are lost in a spiritual wilderness. What are you and your church doing specifically to reach those in the spiritual wasteland?

John the Baptist Prepares for Jesus (1:4–8)

John the Baptist was unusual, even for his day. He was a successor to the Old Testament prophets. His dress and ministry reminded his audience of Elijah (see 2 Kings 1:8). He was bold, even in the face of the wicked King Herod (Mark 6:14–29), which caused his arrest and eventually his execution. Even the religious leaders of the day recognized that the people saw John as a prophet (11:27–33). John the Baptist prepared his hearers for the coming of Jesus by preaching "a baptism of repentance for the forgiveness of sins" (1:4). Ultimately, John had a six-part message: (1) repentance; (2) confession; (3) forgiveness; (4) baptism; (5) focus on Jesus; and (6) baptism of the Holy Spirit.

Repentance is not just a big *I'm sorry* to God. Neither is it merely a sorrowful grief over sin. Each of these is part of repentance, but repentance is more. It requires a complete turn-around of behavior to stop sinning and more importantly to turn to a loving daily fellowship with God. It also requires true *confession,* not a general apology—*I'm sorry, Lord, for all that I have done against you today*—but seeking out each specific sin and honestly acknowledging them before God. This takes time and sincerity, which many Christians fail to give to the Lord. True confession is followed by *forgiveness.* These first three elements of John's preaching are not just for the person who initially accepts Christ as his or her Savior. Salvation is more than a one-time experience. There must be a moment in time that each person accepts Jesus as his or her personal Savior (justification), but salvation is also an on-going process in each believer's life (sanctification), which requires continual repentance, confession, and forgiveness. Sadly, many Christians feel as though they are saved and nothing more is required. Jesus asks more than trusting in him one time in life; Jesus also asks that anyone wanting to follow him should deny self, take up a cross daily, and follow him (Mark 8:34; Luke 9:23).

The last three points of John's message are connected to one another, like the first three. John preached and practiced *baptism.* Although

TO WHOM DO YOU MINISTER?

To which of the following would your church be quicker to minister: (1) a well-dressed, middle-income family of five, who is coming to your church because they are disgruntled with their old one; or (2) the awkward loner who is broken and needy? To which do you think Jesus would be quickest to minister?

baptism is not an Old Testament practice, its roots can be found in the ceremonial cleansing of those deemed unclean (Exodus 19:10; Leviticus 14—16; Numbers 19; Ezekiel 36:25). John's point was that all people are unclean and need to be cleansed before God. John used his baptism to identify those who acknowledged that they were seeking a new life, but then John pointed to Jesus as the one who would bring that new life. John *focused on Jesus* as the way of salvation. The forgiveness of sins had to come through Jesus. John proclaimed that *baptism of the Holy Spirit* would also come. Jesus extended the Holy Spirit into the lives of believers in order that they might have comfort, counsel, and instruction (see John 14:15–17, 25–26; 16:5–15).

John the Baptist Prepares Jesus (1:9–11)

After first preparing the people for Jesus, John assisted in preparing Jesus for his own ministry. As with the first thirty-nine chapters of Isaiah, John's message was a message of repentance and judgment (see Matthew 3:1–17; Luke 3:3–18, 21–23). Jesus would continue to preach the same message but then would become the sacrifice by which God would bring comfort, deliverance, and salvation. Matthew records that John was reluctant to baptize Jesus because John felt unworthy, but Jesus reassured him that it must happen to "fulfill all righteousness" (Matt. 3:14–15). John was preparing Jesus for his ministry by ceremonially cleansing him (even though Jesus was without sin). Jesus was publicly submitting to the will of the Father, accepting the ministry the Father had laid out for him. Likewise, our baptism is a public statement of faith in which we identify with Jesus and demonstrate our submission to the will of God.

Mark 1:10–11 mentions all three persons of the Trinity within two verses, providing the perfect picture of the role of each. The Father spoke from heaven, the incarnate Son stood on Earth, and the Spirit descended from heaven into the world, on God's Chosen One.

The voice of God from heaven declared, "You are my Son, whom I love; with you I am well pleased" (Mark 1:11). The Father validated the deity of Jesus, thus confirming Mark's point in the title that Jesus is the Son of God (1:1). The voice also validated the relationship of the Son to the Father and the role of the Son. The relationship is sealed with a mutual divine love. The Father was pleased with the Son's commitment to fulfilling his role as the Savior of the world.

Implications and Actions

The Gospel of Mark demonstrates how the Scriptures and John the Baptist prepared the world for Jesus. We can be like John in our day and prepare our world for Jesus. There are people in each of our lives who are in a spiritual wasteland and need the comfort, guidance, deliverance, and salvation that only Jesus can bring.

We must present Jesus as the Christ and the Son of God as we talk about Jesus. We live in a world that accepts general spiritual truths but shies away from specific revealed truths like salvation through Jesus or the deity of Jesus. If we accept Jesus as our Christ and if we accept the Bible as the authoritative word of God, we must reveal the Jesus who is revealed within the Bible—the divine Son of God who offers forgiveness to all who believe.

QUESTIONS

1. What does it mean that the entire Book of Mark is only the beginning of the gospel of Jesus?

2. Are you interested in reaching people in the spiritual wilderness like John and Jesus? If so, how are you doing it?

3. Do you live a confessed, repentant life before God on a daily basis?

4. Have you asked for forgiveness of your sins specifically, or do you occasionally ask for forgiveness in a general sense?

5. Who specifically are you preparing for Jesus? How are you preparing him or her?

NOTES

1. See also Mark 13:32.

2. Unless otherwise indicated, all Scripture quotations in lessons 1–6, 10–11 are taken from the HOLY BIBLE, NEW INTERNATIONAL VERSION®. Copyright © 1973, 1978, 1984 Biblica.

LESSON TWO

Peter: Telling Jesus He's Wrong

Likely everyone can remember playing in the school yard when the dilemma arose over choosing sides. Each person eagerly awaited his or her name to be called. No one wanted to be left out. Some kids secretly wanted to be on the same side as a certain leader. Even today, we all want to be included and to feel that we are chosen by others. The fact is we *have* been chosen, by God, to be his disciples. The choosing of the first twelve foreshadows that Jesus chooses all disciples.

MARK 1:16–18

16 As Jesus walked beside the Sea of Galilee, he saw Simon and his brother Andrew casting a net into the lake, for they were fishermen. 17 "Come, follow me," Jesus said, "and I will make you fishers of men." 18 At once they left their nets and followed him.

MARK 8:27–33

27 Jesus and his disciples went on to the villages around Caesarea Philippi. On the way he asked them, "Who do people say I am?"

28 They replied, "Some say John the Baptist; others say Elijah; and still others, one of the prophets."

29 "But what about you?" he asked. "Who do you say I am?" Peter answered, "You are the Christ."

30 Jesus warned them not to tell anyone about him.

31 He then began to teach them that the Son of Man must suffer many things and be rejected by the elders, chief priests and teachers of the law, and that he must be killed and after three days rise again.

32 He spoke plainly about this, and Peter took him aside and began to rebuke him.

33 But when Jesus turned and looked at his disciples, he rebuked Peter. "Get behind me, Satan!" he said. "You do not have in mind the things of God, but the things of men."

MARK 14:26–31, 66–72

26 When they had sung a hymn, they went out to the Mount of Olives.

27 "You will all fall away," Jesus told them, "for it is written:

"'I will strike the shepherd, and the sheep will be scattered.'

28 But after I have risen, I will go ahead of you into Galilee."

29 Peter declared, "Even if all fall away, I will not."

30 "I tell you the truth," Jesus answered, "today—yes, tonight—before the rooster crows twice you yourself will disown me three times."

31 But Peter insisted emphatically, "Even if I have to die with you, I will never disown you." And all the others said the same.

• •

66 While Peter was below in the courtyard, one of the servant girls of the high priest came by. 67 When she saw Peter warming himself, she looked closely at him.

"You also were with that Nazarene, Jesus," she said.

68 But he denied it. "I don't know or understand what you're talking about," he said, and went out into the entryway.

69 When the servant girl saw him there, she said again to those standing around, "This fellow is one of them." 70 Again he denied it.

After a little while, those standing near said to Peter, "Surely you are one of them, for you are a Galilean."

71 He began to call down curses on himself, and he swore to them, "I don't know this man you're talking about."

72 Immediately the rooster crowed the second time. Then Peter remembered the word Jesus had spoken to him: "Before the rooster crows twice you will disown me three times." And he broke down and wept.

MARK 16:5–7

5 As they entered the tomb, they saw a young man dressed in a white robe sitting on the right side, and they were alarmed.

> [6] "Don't be alarmed," he said. "You are looking for Jesus the Nazarene, who was crucified. He has risen! He is not here. See the place where they laid him. [7] But go, tell his disciples and Peter, 'He is going ahead of you into Galilee. There you will see him, just as he told you.'"

Jesus Chose Peter as a Disciple (1:16–18)

Jesus chose Peter, and not the other way around. Mark wrote that Peter was at work one day when Jesus immediately called to Peter to follow. Mark focused on the speed by which Jesus chose his disciples and by which they responded. The other Gospels give more details, but the calling from Jesus was certainly a quick one (see Luke 5:1–11; John 1:35–42; see also Mark 10:28). Jesus was walking along the seashore when he called Peter, Andrew, James, and John, as if to say he did not even stop and was choosing them suddenly and in mid-stride. Their response was equally quick and immediate. Simon (soon to be called Peter, Mark 3:13–16) and Andrew "at once . . . left their nets and followed him" (1:18). Leaving their nets also indicates that following Jesus was costly to Peter and Andrew. They gave up their livelihood as regular fishermen to become disciples of Jesus. It was a significant commitment, and yet they made it without deliberation or delay. They committed to Jesus immediately.

Mark's Gospel moves at a fast pace, but it also emphasizes that would-be disciples must be certain of the commitment they are making to Jesus. Perhaps Jesus called others who refused to get up and follow him. Jesus did not beg or plead with anyone to follow him. At times, he seemed to make it difficult. One scribe committed to follow him, "Teacher I will follow you wherever you go." Jesus responded, "Foxes have holes and birds of the air have nests, but the Son of Man has no place to lay his head" (Matt. 8:19–20). He also told a rich man, "Go, sell everything you have and give to the poor, and you will have treasure in heaven. Then come, follow me" (Mark 10:21).

Jesus is still calling disciples today with the same combination of urgency but seriousness. Has your response been like Peter's, immediate and costly? Or if you were honest, would you say that your discipleship is conditional, based on whether it suits your needs?

Peter Told Jesus He Was Wrong About God's Plan (8:27–33)

There is a dramatic shift in these seven short verses. In the first half, verses 27–29, Peter acknowledged that Jesus is the Christ. In the second half, verses 30–33, Jesus rebuked Peter and seemed to call him Satan. The pivotal point in the narrative came when Peter in essence told Jesus he was wrong about God's plan.

Jesus inquired what the crowd thought about him. The disciples had a good understanding of what the rumors were. They knew that the masses felt Jesus was a special prophet, maybe John the Baptist, Elijah, or someone else, but Jesus wanted more from his disciples. Jesus is greater than all the prophets. Jesus was not the forerunner of the Christ, but rather he was indeed the Christ. Mark 1:1 declares that the gospel includes this very point, that Jesus is the Christ. No one had acknowledged that yet within Mark's Gospel.

Jesus directed the question of what the masses thought of him to the more personal question, "But what about you? . . . Who do you say I am?" (Mark 8:29). Finally Peter provided the answer that Mark had been setting up within his Gospel all along when Peter answered Jesus, "You are the Christ." Jesus allowed his disciples to come to this conclusion themselves. Likewise, Jesus wants us to come to the conclusion as to who we think he is. And then we must answer him just as Peter did.

Jesus immediately told Peter, who might have been speaking on behalf of all the disciples, to tell no one this secret. Jesus was not quite ready for the world to know he was the Christ. He knew everyone was not ready and that the response of the general population would work against God's real plan. Based on the response of the disciples, he was right.

What mix of pride and joy must have flooded Peter's heart when Jesus confirmed with a quick nod that Peter had answered correctly! Finally the long-awaited Christ was on Earth and in Peter's presence. Moreover, Peter was the person who identified the Christ first. Maybe Peter understood Jesus' request to keep it a secret, or maybe not. But Jesus' order to Peter to keep his identity secret served only to heighten the privileged information Peter then possessed.

Then suddenly the tenor of the conversation changed drastically. Once the disciples knew Jesus was indeed the Christ, Jesus began to reveal to them the details of the plan of God for them. He shared he was going to suffer, be rejected, killed, but come back to life. Peter did not like the sound of the plan Jesus was laying out, and so he rebuked Jesus. Jesus in return rebuked Peter. This was not a minor argument. "Rebuke" means a heated argument with raised voices and emotions running hot. Peter's joy had turned to anger, which only incited Jesus to return with his strongest words uttered to any disciple, "Get behind me, Satan!" (8:33). Jesus had explained all of this in detail and with great deliberation—"He spoke plainly about this." There was no mistaking what Jesus had said to his disciples. Peter's response was a direct objection to this plan laid out by Jesus. Jesus responded so harshly for four reasons: (1) to correct the false beliefs the disciples had about him and his role; (2) to keep the disciples in line "behind" him so they could truly follow him; (3) to bring focus back on the will of God; and (4) to counter the work of Satan. Consider each reason.

(1) Jesus was correcting the false image the disciples had built up in their minds about him. Is it possible that many disciples today have a false notion of who Jesus really is? Perhaps they have imagined and created a Jesus who fits their plans and desires, only to have missed who the real Jesus is all along.

(2) Jesus' charge to "get behind me" can be interpreted in at least two ways. One view is that Jesus was talking to Satan, commanding Satan to get out of the way. Could it be, though, that he was talking to the disciples, Peter in particular? Mark used the motif of Jesus saying, "Follow me," throughout his Gospel. Too, even in the temptation experience recorded in Mark 1:13, Jesus did not command Satan, "Get behind me." So it seems that Jesus was talking to his disciples and telling them to fall in line, "behind" him.

(3) Although Jesus clearly told the disciples what God's plan was, Peter was rejecting it because he did not like it. How often do we reject God's will for our lives or in the lives of our loved ones because it does not meet our sensibilities for the world in which we live. Parents may try to dissuade a child from committing to missions or ministry because the child had the gifts *to do great things*. Christians try to avoid suffering or hardships that are too uncomfortable even though they might be part of God's overall plan to reach others. Jesus' rebuke goes to anyone who forsakes the will of God when it is tough.

PETER

In Mark 3:16, Jesus changed Simon's name to "Peter." "Peter" is the English version of the Greek word *petros,* which means *rock.* The Aramaic version is *kepa,* which is transliterated to English as *Cephas.* The New Testament was written in Greek, and so Christians are more familiar with the Greek version (and its derivatives). However, Jesus almost certainly spoke Aramaic, which means he would have called Simon "Cephas" instead of "Peter." The Apostle John, who walked with both of them, referred to the Aramaic version first and then explained the Greek for his readers (John 1:42). Paul also referred to him as Cephas eight times, demonstrating that he also knew Peter by the Aramaic name (1 Corinthians 1:12; 3:21; 9:5; 15:5; Galatians 1:18; 2:9). Mark was writing to the church in Rome, which had been under the leadership of Peter, and so he used the Greek name Peter, by which Peter had then become known better.

(4) Jesus was countering the work of Satan in one of two ways, or both: (a) he was indirectly countering the work of Satan as much as Satan had influenced Peter; and/or (b) he was speaking directly to Satan. In the former, Jesus might very well have been calling Peter "Satan" because Peter was demonstrating the age-old sin of trying to twist out of the will of God. In the latter, Jesus was directly addressing Satan, who was still trying to thwart the will of God.

Peter Told Jesus He Was Wrong About Peter's Commitment (14:26–31, 66–72)

Peter repeated his mistake the night Jesus was arrested. Jesus was once again providing more details to the plan of God for the events that would unfold in the hours to come. He told his disciples they would fall away that evening and all become deserters. That had to be unthinkable to all of them. They had given up so much to follow Jesus and yet he then doubted them? Peter once again told Jesus that Jesus was wrong. Peter felt his commitment to Christ was far superior to that of anyone else. He was probably very earnest in his heart and was confident that he

TELLING JESUS HE IS WRONG BY OUR ACTIONS

We tell Jesus he is wrong

- About providing for us, when we worry
- About his plan for our lives, when we ignore it
- About the Holy Spirit comforting and counseling us, when we don't recognize him
- About the importance of Scripture, when we don't read it and pay attention to it
- About the reality of Satan, when we deny Satan's attempts to tempt us
- About Jesus' love and forgiveness, when we live in our past failures

would die with Jesus if he had to. Jesus knew he was overly confident and not able to see his own weakness. He knew that Peter would fail, too, just as the others. Jesus predicted a very specific desertion by Peter that included not one but three denials of knowing Jesus. He then gave Peter a sign to govern his denial, the morning's crowing rooster.

Mark 14:66–72 records Peter's own personal failure. Of course it happened as Jesus said it would. The third denial coincided with the second rooster's crow. In sorrow, "he broke down and wept." Surely, Peter remembered this terrible night for the rest of his life every time he heard a rooster crow. He had claimed Jesus was wrong about his commitment, but Peter turned out to be the one who was wrong. How often have we been like Peter, so secure while in the moment with God that we would do all that God desires, only to find failure lurking around the corner?

Jesus Still Wanted Peter to Be a Disciple (16:5–7)

Peter failed Jesus, as did everyone else. He had the haunting memory of denying his master, the one Peter knew was the Christ. Could there be any redemption for him? Jesus was tortured and then crucified and

Peter failed him through it all! Yet, Mark 16:5–7 provides two of the most wonderful thoughts Peter could have ever imagined—*Jesus is alive!* and *Jesus wants to see you, Peter.* Peter did indeed experience full redemption. Jesus extended his love to Peter in spite of Peter's failure.

Implications and Actions

We can be like Peter and reject God's will for our lives (or the lives of our loved ones), and we can be like Peter, overlooking our weakness and then falling to temptation. We must constantly look to Christ to guide us in our daily walk. Many people feel as though they have failed God so badly that redemption is not possible for them. Like Peter who went from sorrow to being redeemed, God is always ready to redeem his people, through Jesus' death. Although there still may be lingering effects of our sin, God still loves us, and the living Jesus awaits our coming to him.

QUESTIONS

1. Have you accepted what Jesus has called you to do in your walk with him?

2. Who do you say Jesus is? What does that mean?

3. Have you ever said *no* to God because you didn't understand what God was doing or because you didn't like what God was doing? Will you confess that to God and be willing to submit to his will regardless of what it may bring?

4. Have you denied Christ in a public setting before? Have you down-played your faith? Will you confess that too and make the commitment to be bold about your faith?

FOCAL TEXT
Mark 1:19–20; 3:13–
17; 10:35–45

BACKGROUND
Mark 1:16–20, 29;
3:13–17; 5:35–37; 9:2–8;
10:35–45; 14:32–42

MAIN IDEA

Even though James and John
had left much behind to
follow Jesus, they continued
to need Jesus' correction
and instruction about
serving him and others.

QUESTION TO EXPLORE

What do you yet have to learn
about serving Jesus and others?

STUDY AIM

To trace the relationship
of James and John to Jesus
in the Gospel of Mark and
to decide how I will live in
accord with Jesus' teaching
about servanthood

QUICK READ

James and John were interested
in being leaders for Christ.
Jesus was more interested
in them being servants.

LESSON THREE
James and John: We Are First

When I was a new pastor I attended a local pastors' conference fairly regularly. Over time I noticed many of the other pastors seemed to ask the same questions, *How many people did you have in Sunday School? Are your tithes keeping up? How many baptisms have you had in the past year?* I do not fault these pastors; their questions were normal to them in checking on one another (mostly in a sincere way).

One man stood out as different: Pastor James. He was interested in my walk with Christ and the ministry we could do together to benefit the kingdom of heaven. He wasn't just interested in ecclesiastical accounting or self-measuring. He had a constant humility about him. I was aware that the people within his church knew he loved them and that he was totally committed to his ministry as their pastor. Later I learned that he and his wife had lost each of their two teenage children within months of each other about ten years earlier. Their son died with cancer, and then their daughter was killed in a traffic accident. Pastor James did not care much about what others thought was so very important in church work. He cared about serving the people God had given to him to serve as pastor.

Likewise, James and John (and presumably the other disciples) cared about things Jesus did not care about. Jesus knew what was truly important. He called his disciples to follow him, which ultimately leads to a life of service.

MARK 1:19–20

19 When he had gone a little farther, he saw James son of Zebedee and his brother John in a boat, preparing their nets. 20 Without delay he called them, and they left their father Zebedee in the boat with the hired men and followed him.

MARK 3:13–17

13 Jesus went up on a mountainside and called to him those he wanted, and they came to him. 14 He appointed twelve— designating them apostles—that they might be with him and that he might send them out to preach 15 and to have authority to drive out demons. 16 These are the twelve he appointed: Simon (to whom he gave the name Peter); 17 James son of Zebedee and his

brother John (to them he gave the name Boanerges, which means Sons of Thunder);

MARK 10:35–45

35 Then James and John, the sons of Zebedee, came to him. "Teacher," they said, "we want you to do for us whatever we ask."

36 "What do you want me to do for you?" he asked.

37 They replied, "Let one of us sit at your right and the other at your left in your glory."

38 "You don't know what you are asking," Jesus said. "Can you drink the cup I drink or be baptized with the baptism I am baptized with?"

39 "We can," they answered.

Jesus said to them, "You will drink the cup I drink and be baptized with the baptism I am baptized with, 40 but to sit at my right or left is not for me to grant. These places belong to those for whom they have been prepared."

41 When the ten heard about this, they became indignant with James and John. 42 Jesus called them together and said, "You know that those who are regarded as rulers of the Gentiles lord it over them, and their high officials exercise authority over them. 43 Not so with you. Instead, whoever wants to become great among you must be your servant, 44 and whoever wants to be first must be slave of all. 45 For even the Son of Man did not come to be served, but to serve, and to give his life as a ransom for many."

Being a Disciple of Jesus Is a Privilege (1:19–20; 3:13–17)

Jesus' calling of all of his disciples was one of privilege. In Mark 1:19–20, the response of James and John to Jesus' calling in their lives was immediate. They willingly left their father's business to follow Jesus. It is even easy to imagine that as they were in the middle of repairing nets, they literally dropped what they were doing and left their unfinished work to the other hired men in the boat.

The initial decision by James and John to follow Jesus came at a steep price. Although Peter and Andrew also left their vocation as fishermen, James and John were the sons of the owner of the fishing business. In addition to leaving their jobs as Peter and Andrew did, they left their father and their inheritance all in one moment. Yet, they still had a great privilege to walk with Jesus throughout his earthly ministry.

Usually, disciples chose which rabbi they would follow. Jesus' choosing the Twelve was a great honor. Jesus constantly had dozens, hundreds, and even thousands surrounding him. In Mark 3:13–19, Jesus, however, pulled away from the clustered followers, moved up on a mountainside, and started calling the names one by one, *Simon, James, John. . . .* What a privilege! Jesus even gave the brothers a combined nickname, "Sons of Thunder" (literally, *the loud ones*), indicating the closeness he shared with them. Although this nickname is never explained, it is obvious that these two were vocal leaders.

Jesus further designated these Twelve as his "apostles," which indicates that they were being sent out instead of just called to learn from Jesus. They were being sent for two purposes: "to preach and to have

BAPTISM

Baptism is an important part of Christianity in general and Baptist heritage in particular. Yet, Jesus referred to baptism in Mark 10:35–45 as a metaphor. He was not talking about the Christian ordinance of baptism. In fact, the Gospels don't have a lot to say about baptism. Although John's baptism of Jesus is recorded, the apostles' baptisms aren't. Nowhere in the Gospels is it said that baptism is necessary for salvation.

Putting what the Gospels say about baptism with what they do not say leads to a basic understanding of the ordinance. Baptism is a very important part of discipleship that demonstrates obedience. Since it is not a requirement for salvation, baptism becomes the free expression of commitment to Jesus Christ. Matthew finished his Gospel with a command to go into the world making disciples and baptizing people from all nations (Matthew 28:19), emphasizing its importance.

authority over demons" (Mark 3:15). Jesus continued to narrow the privileges he had given to his disciples. More than just being called to Jesus, the apostles were called to serve specific roles.

Today, we should still consider being a disciple of Jesus as a privilege. After all, Jesus still chooses his disciples (not the other way around). In John 6:44, Jesus reminds us that "no one can come to me unless the Father who sent me draws him. . . ." How often do we take our discipleship for granted? Our salvation is a great work of grace in our life and a free gift from God.

We have been called to Jesus, but that is not the end of the matter for us either. We are also called to serve Jesus' purposes in specific roles.

Jesus' Disciples Are Called to Submit (10:35–41)

James and John sought to be first among the apostles. They were trying to put themselves in a place of power since Jesus would soon reveal his role as the Christ. Jesus' response was complex as it revealed that their request was misguided. Jesus gave a fourfold response.

(1) "You don't know what you are asking." James and John certainly had a different expectation of what was about to happen in the immediate future than was the plan of God. Perhaps they were expecting a new earthly kingdom in Jerusalem with Jesus as the king and they at his side, but, of course, God's plan was for Jesus to be executed within the next few days. Often, we are too much like James and John. When we allow our ideas and desires to take priority in our lives instead of seeking what God's plan is, our prayer lives can become as futile as the request of the brothers to be first in the kingdom of Jesus.

(2) "Can you drink the cup I drink?" Jesus used two metaphors to describe what he was about to do. The first, "the cup," is found throughout the Old Testament. "Cup" refers to the goodness and blessing from God in some scriptural instances, but in the majority, it is a reference to judgment, sorrow, suffering, and death. Jesus was definitely speaking in the general sense of his upcoming suffering and death. He was also specifically referring to "the cup" of salvation he would lift within a few days at Passover when he said at the Last Supper, "This is my blood of the covenant, which is poured out for many" (14:23–24), as he passed it to these very disciples and had them

to drink after him. Even though in Mark 10:39, Jesus allowed them some latitude in sharing in this cup, they could never be the ransom for many that Jesus was (10:45). Jesus challenged their understanding of what his kingdom would be.

There is a current within Christianity that portrays faith in Christ as a stepping stone to wealth and blessing in this life. Jesus did not present such a plan. Rather Jesus commands his disciples to be ready to deny self and take up a cross as he did.

(3) "Can you . . . be baptized with the baptism I am baptized with?" Jesus used the metaphor of baptism to refer to the overwhelming flood-like experience he was about to endure. He was not referring to his or the disciples baptismal experience. Additionally, Jesus was not going to be baptized a second time. Rather Jesus was speaking of the deluge of difficulty and sorrow he would experience in the next week, both physically as well as spiritually. He would carry the burden of the sins of all who would believe in him. Jesus' words reflected the heaviness of his heart as he neared the moment of his sacrifice in contrast to the brothers' desire to be first in the kingdom.

(4) Jesus' expression of limitation (10:40) indicates that even Jesus was not able to part from the divine plan. His statement that he did not have the right to grant who sits to his left and right may seem somewhat strange. After all, the point of Mark is that Jesus is the Son of God. The kingdom Jesus was establishing was his own kingdom. Why would he not have the right to grant who does what? Jesus limited his own prerogative within his earthly reign for three reasons: (a) to establish the providence and superiority of the divine purposes that are already at work; (b) to demonstrate that God's purposes will not be thwarted; (c) to demonstrate Jesus' own submission to the plan of God (to be "a ransom for many"). He needed to cling to these as he entered the dark period of God's plan. If Jesus was willing to submit to the will of God, then so should all of his disciples, beginning with James and John and extending all the way to all of us.

Jesus' Disciples Are Called to Serve (10:42–45)

The other ten apostles "became indignant with James and John" (10:41). Jesus took the opportunity to address them all. He used the illustration of government rulers to indicate the type of leader he would be and what he expected of them. Mark's original audience of the Christians in Rome would have been as equally amazed as Jesus' disciples as to the type of hierarchy Jesus was establishing. Jesus' negation, "not so with you" (10:43), immediately fostered the question, *Then how shall we rule?* Jesus gave the most unexpected answer, *You won't!*

Jesus gave a two-fold plan of Christian leadership. (1) Those who would like to be great must become servants. The Greek word for servant is *diakonos*, from which the word *deacon* comes. It did not have any greater meaning than simply "servant." Jesus was not establishing a hierarchy within church leadership, but rather he was emphasizing that to be great within Jesus' kingdom, one has to serve in much the same way as a household servant would serve. The apostles (and Mark's readers) would have found this difficult to accept and quite shocking. The fact that the shock has worn off somewhat for us may mean the contemporary church needs to revisit Jesus' teaching on being servants, including would-be Christian leaders being servants.

(2) Jesus went further in his instructions on Christian leadership by making an even more shocking comment. If those who want to be great must become servants (*diakonos*), then those who want to be first must lower themselves even more to become slaves (*doulos*) of all. If a servant had any rights, privileges, or expectations, slaves had none. Slaves were seen as little more than livestock in the ancient Roman world. Jesus was answering James and John by saying, *You want to be first? Then relinquish any rights, privileges, or expectations, and begin to serve everyone else.* What a word of warning to Christian leaders who can fall into the temptation of self-importance and the desire to "lord it over" their churches and ministries. Jesus was saying that Christian fellowship does not exist for its leaders, but Christian leaders exist for the fellowship. More importantly, Jesus provided the ultimate example to this message as he gave his life for all sinners, "while we were still sinners" (Romans 5:8b).

Implications and Actions

We live in an age when power, prestige, authority, and control can reign in the church as much as in the secular world. Churches are marketing and branding themselves in very nearly the same way as businesses. Sometimes it is difficult to distinguish between a senior pastor and a CEO. Denominations are wrestling for control of institutions, leadership, and reputations.

Jesus told his very first disciples to remember to be servants and slaves. All Christians need to resist the temptation of James and John to strive for personal recognition and control. We must recognize that our call into discipleship is a privilege and that Jesus has called us to submit to God's plan for us and to serve others in the way that Jesus himself did.

QUESTIONS

1. Do you understand what a privilege you have in being a disciple of Jesus?

2. Have you been confused as to what God's plan was at some point in your life? Did you submit to God anyway, or were you more interested in fulfilling your wishes?

3. What does it mean to you that even Jesus limited himself in what he could grant to his disciples?

4. Can you honestly say that you are a servant to the fellow people of God in your church? Would you go so far as to think of yourself as a slave to them? If not, why not?

5. Would you honestly describe your spirit more like the humility demonstrated by Jesus or the ambition of James and John?

FOCAL TEXT
Mark 2:13–17

BACKGROUND
Mark 2:13–17

MAIN IDEA

Jesus openly accepted Levi and other people like him even though the religious leaders considered them outsiders and unacceptable.

QUESTION TO EXPLORE

Does the gospel really mean we should accept *those* people?

STUDY AIM

To describe Levi's relationship to Jesus and to decide how I will follow Jesus' model in reaching out to and accepting people often considered outsiders and unacceptable

QUICK READ

Although some did not accept Jesus' acceptance of and compassion for all people, that did not deter Jesus in his mission.

LESSON FOUR
Levi: Outsiders Welcome

Our Sunday School teacher said, "You've probably heard this before, and this is not an exact quote, but consider these words: There's so much good in the worst of us and so much bad in the best of us that it behooves none of us to talk about the rest of us." He paused and then said, "Remember my version: there's so much good in the worst of us and so much bad in the best of us that it behooves none of us to draw lines where God does not." My teacher accomplished his purpose. I remember the words decades later, for they touched my life.

MARK 2:13–17

¹³ Once again Jesus went out beside the lake. A large crowd came to him, and he began to teach them. ¹⁴ As he walked along, he saw Levi son of Alphaeus sitting at the tax collector's booth. "Follow me," Jesus told him, and Levi got up and followed him.

¹⁵ While Jesus was having dinner at Levi's house, many tax collectors and "sinners" were eating with him and his disciples, for there were many who followed him. ¹⁶ When the teachers of the law who were Pharisees saw him eating with the "sinners" and tax collectors, they asked his disciples: "Why does he eat with tax collectors and 'sinners'?"

¹⁷ On hearing this, Jesus said to them, "It is not the healthy who need a doctor, but the sick. I have not come to call the righteous, but sinners."

Stepping Outside the Lines (2:13–14)

Jewish society in Jesus' day drew lines clearly. Jews and Gentiles knew where the lines were drawn. Men and women knew the lines. Children had the boundaries embedded in them from an early age. Rules abounded, and people were taught that the way to get right with God and get along in the world was to obey the rules and traditions as taught by the religious leaders. Some of that attitude still persists in our world today.

Jesus had already called four disciples to follow him (Mark 1:16–20). He was teaching the masses of people, but he also saw individuals in the crowd surrounding him. "Once again," the Scripture says, Jesus was walking and teaching. This time he saw an individual, Levi, who was a tax collector. Jesus said to Levi what Jesus had told Peter, Andrew, James, and John: "Follow me." Such a simple plan. Perhaps each of these five had earlier heard Jesus speak or watched him, but Jesus used no icebreaker or offered no incentives. "Follow me." That still defines us in relationship to Jesus. We are to follow him.

Jesus' choice of Levi (known to us also as Matthew) would have stunned the crowds. They probably had seen Levi at his small booth or office, collecting taxes on commerce being transported through Capernaum. He probably represented Herod Antipas, the ruler of the area. By evening, Capernaum must have been buzzing about Levi being Jesus' latest recruit. Choosing some fishermen, even if they didn't always get the rules right, was one thing, but choosing a tax collector? People would have been stunned, for tax collectors were considered the scum of Jewish society. They were notorious for taking more than they were supposed to collect. Jesus crossed the lines the Jewish religious leaders had drawn. To them, Jesus had stepped way beyond the boundaries.

Notice what Jesus noticed: "As he walked along, he saw Levi." Often we lose sight of the individual. A crowd, many of whom might have been unknown even to one another, might have blurred the identity of an individual, but Jesus saw Levi. Perhaps you have had the experience in a store of bumping into someone, and one of you said, *I'm sorry; I didn't see you.* That might have been true, but at a deeper level, we often do not *see* others. Read some eternal consequences of that blindness in Matthew 25:31–46.

Levi's response to Jesus was simple: "Levi got up and followed him." Probably you remember playing *follow the leader* as a child. Jesus used that idea in a more significant way. The essence of faith is to follow Jesus. For Levi, that choice might not have been as easy as it was for the first four disciples Jesus chose. They could always go back to fishing, but Levi might not have been able to return to his "tax collector's booth" once he had left it. Levi had taken a dramatic step. He got in line behind Jesus. Later, he would have the privilege of writing the story of Jesus, but first there was a time to celebrate with his friends.

Dinner Table Evangelism (2:15)

Pay careful attention to Levi's model of evangelism. When Levi started following Jesus, he threw a party. Levi invited his friends, most of whom would have been other "tax collectors and 'sinners.'" Excluded from the company of many of the religious people in the first century, tax collectors and sinners were about all that was left for Levi. However, he wanted his friends to meet Jesus. Apparently, some already had, but so many others needed to meet Jesus as well.

Most of us have had enjoyable dinner table conversations ended by, *Let's go somewhere more comfortable to talk.* Maybe it works in many cases, but often the words do not flow as freely as they had been flowing around the table. Don't neglect the dinner table as an opportunity to celebrate happy occasions. Celebrate baptisms and any other spiritual events around the table, and invite some people who would have no knowledge of what happens at a baptism or church event. Also, don't forget the table as a place to introduce unchurched or unsaved people to some of your Christian friends. Before they feel comfortable in your church pew, they may need to know Christian friends around your dinner table and in your home. Maybe invite your pastor also; my guess is your pastor would like a casual atmosphere to spend time with you and any of your friends. In some way, Jesus might show up too!

Proper People Demand Why (2:16)

On several occasions in Mark 2, the "why" questions are asked. After Jesus healed the paralytic, the religious leaders asked, "Why does this fellow [Jesus] talk like that?" (Mark 2:7). Although they should have been amazed by Jesus healing a crippled man, they were shocked that Jesus claimed he could forgive the man's sins. Others were truly amazed, though, saying, "We have never seen anything like this!" (2:12).

At Levi's house, the Pharisees tried to get the disciples to rein Jesus in, asking, "Why does he eat with tax collectors and 'sinners'?" (2:16). They assumed that everyone should know that God has nothing to do with *those kind* of people. Later, others wanted Jesus to explain why his disciples did not fast (2:18) and why the disciples violated the Sabbath laws by plucking grain on the Sabbath (2:24).

No answer would suffice these critics because any answer would take them outside the rules and boundaries they had already established. The lines were drawn, and they were sure their lines were God's lines. They

OUTSIDERS IN THE CHRISTMAS STORY

The Gospel of Mark begins with the public ministry of Jesus and has no record of his birth. Although Matthew's Gospel had specific appeal to a Jewish-Christian audience, Matthew also reveals God's love for common people and outsiders. God used two people from an insignificant small town of Nazareth to become earthly parents of Jesus (Matt. 1:18–25). Some of the first visitors to see Jesus were foreigners who traveled a great distance to pay homage to him. We call them *wise men* (Matt. 2:1–11). In Luke, the lowest class of citizens (shepherds) was the first to hear about the birth of Jesus (Luke 2:1–20). In the Gospel of John, it is said of Jesus, "He came to that which was his own, but his own did not receive him" (John 1:11). In a sense, Jesus was both an insider and an outsider to Jewish society, but his mission and ministry was to reach and include all people—outsiders as well as insiders.

were sure they had the truth, the whole truth, and nothing but the truth. As they continued to harass Jesus, they became increasingly agitated at the popularity of Jesus and their inability to confound his arguments. Legalists in any age tend to have little patience.

Keep in mind the Pharisees. They began as a lay movement in the interbiblical period, and their patriotism and spiritual commitment probably helped Judaism to survive during some difficult days. Even though they became entrenched in their ways, they were not enemies from Jesus' point of view. He ate in their homes as well as in Levi's home. He talked with them privately and publicly. It was not Jesus' will that many of them remained hostile to him. They too were "sinners" (although they might have argued that point), and they too needed Jesus as their Savior. Proper religious people can be just as lost and needy as the worst sinner that they would disdain.

A rereading of the story of the prodigal son and the elder brother would be appropriate here (Luke 15:1–2, 11–32). Note the circumstances that inspired the great story. Keep praying for all sinners, including the religious or irreligious ones, which would include you and me as well.

DRAWING LINES

In the eyes of many in the first-century world, Jesus brought an *outsider* of the worst sort—indeed, a *scumbag*—into the inner circle of disciples when he called Levi to follow him. Later another tax collector, Zacchaeus (Luke 19:1–10), became a follower of Jesus. Since these outsiders were representative of people who were often ostracized by religious people and perhaps fellow disciples in the first century, what implications does that have for our evangelism and fellowship in the twenty-first century? Where do we draw lines that we choose not to cross in relating to others? As a follower of Jesus, why?

Bringing Health to the Sick (2:17)

The healing ministry of Jesus is spotlighted in many places in the Gospel of Mark. Jesus healed the demon-possessed man, a leper, a paralytic, a sick woman, a deaf and mute man, a blind man, a young boy, and many others. He brought Jairus's twelve-year-old daughter to life again. Jesus healed many people.

In verse 17, Jesus used the healing metaphor to describe his spiritual ministry. His critics asked, "Why does he eat with tax collectors and 'sinners'?" (Mark 2:16). Jesus' answer was framed as a doctor-patient relationship. The doctor's concern is, *Where are the sick?* When the doctor enters a room, the doctor's concern is with the sick person. Jesus said that was what he was here to do—bring wholeness and healing to those who are sinners.

Jesus' critics would have thought themselves to be righteous, in no real need of healing. They would have also assumed they did not need a Savior. They believed that being a child of God was their birthright as Jews. Furthermore, their relationship with God was sealed, for they kept the law as they understood and refined it. For Jesus' critics, people like Levi were beyond hope, for they were sinners. In truth, the Pharisee was a sick patient, and so was the tax collector. Both also were sinners. However, if people do not acknowledge the need and sinfulness of their lives, then the doctor is of no avail. Spiritually, no one can force you to go to the spiritual doctor; that is a choice. The Pharisees chose ways that led them away from Jesus while the sinners and tax collectors had an openness to Jesus that others did not.

Did Jesus think the Pharisees were righteous? No. Most likely, Jesus was using sarcasm as a way of making his point. Looking at the question differently, can righteous people look down on others in a despicable manner? Unfortunately, history has more than one example of people professing to be Christians while still having unChristlike attitudes and actions toward others. In a broader application, be careful if you tend to condemn others, for you too may be drawing lines where God does not.

Implications and Actions

The early church's struggle with two questions is found in Acts and the letters of the New Testament: (1) Who can be saved? and (2) With whom do saved people associate? These issues were not solved by Peter's vision in Acts 10 or the decision of the Jerusalem council in Acts 15. In fact, they still persist among Christians today.

Jesus' choice of Levi to become a significant leader in carrying on his mission to the ends of the earth is good news about both salvation and fellowship. The good news that was in Jesus and that is preached about him has a *whosoever will* quality to it. For that to be authentic, we should follow our leader Jesus, become an example of what it means to be saved by grace, and then share that grace with others. Strangely enough, even after 2000 years, we may draw lines or embrace attitudes that keep people from experiencing the saving and life-changing presence of Jesus.

QUESTIONS

1. Why do churches have a difficult time attracting visitors who may be considered "tax collectors and 'sinners'" in our world today?

2. What specifically can your Sunday School class do to help involve *outsiders* in your fellowship and Bible study activities?

3. If your class were to identify three people who are the most welcoming and kind to strangers, including outsiders, would your name be on the list? Why or why not?

4. If following Jesus is used to define our identity as Christians, what does that mean for the way you deal with people who are different racially, socially, or theologically from you?

5. The Latin word for *priest* is a compound word meaning *bridge builder*. How do you fit that definition?

FOCAL TEXT
Mark 5:1–20

BACKGROUND
Mark 5:1–20

MAIN IDEA

Jesus freed a disturbed man from being out of control and sent the man home to tell what Jesus had done for him.

QUESTION TO EXPLORE

From what do you need to let Jesus free you?

STUDY AIM

To describe the radical change Jesus brought to the disturbed man's life and to identify how and from what I need to let Jesus free me

QUICK READ

Jesus healed a man possessed by a demon and freed him for a mission of telling others what God had done in his life.

LESSON FIVE

A Disturbed Man: Freed from Being Out of Control

How did you hear about Jesus? You may be like me—I never remember not knowing about Jesus. From birth, my life was linked with the church through a family that never asked, *Are we going to church this Sunday?* We knew we were going. At the age of ten, I responded in faith to accept Jesus as my Lord and Savior. I recall a couple of significant changes when that happened. First, I stopped sleeping in church. (My parents probably regretted that, and you may still be working on that yourself or in your family.) Second, I wanted others to know about Jesus. I was no crusading evangelist, but I had a sincere desire for others to know about Jesus.

The demon-possessed man in our Scripture for this lesson had a much more dramatic change in life than most of us have had. That does not take away from your or my experience with God. We find similar parallels in the experience of Paul on the Damascus Road (Acts 9:1–8). He also had a life-changing experience that was uniquely his. Although we may have had a different experience from the Gerasene demoniac or Paul, each person's encounter with Jesus is special. We are thankful for a God who makes it possible for us to have a meaningful relationship with him on earth, and who continues with us until we relocate to spend eternity with God in heaven.

MARK 5:1–20

[1] They went across the lake to the region of the Gerasenes. [2] When Jesus got out of the boat, a man with an evil spirit came from the tombs to meet him. [3] This man lived in the tombs, and no one could bind him any more, not even with a chain. [4] For he had often been chained hand and foot, but he tore the chains apart and broke the irons on his feet. No one was strong enough to subdue him. [5] Night and day among the tombs and in the hills he would cry out and cut himself with stones.

[6] When he saw Jesus from a distance, he ran and fell on his knees in front of him. [7] He shouted at the top of his voice, "What do you want with me, Jesus, Son of the Most High God? Swear to God that you won't torture me!" [8] For Jesus had said to him, "Come out of this man, you evil spirit!"

[9] Then Jesus asked him, "What is your name?"

"My name is Legion," he replied, "for we are many." [10] And he begged Jesus again and again not to send them out of the area. [11] A large herd of pigs was feeding on the nearby hillside. [12] The demons begged Jesus, "Send us among the pigs; allow us to go into them." [13] He gave them permission, and the evil spirits came out and went into the pigs. The herd, about two thousand in number, rushed down the steep bank into the lake and were drowned.

[14] Those tending the pigs ran off and reported this in the town and countryside, and the people went out to see what had happened. [15] When they came to Jesus, they saw the man who had been possessed by the legion of demons, sitting there, dressed and in his right mind; and they were afraid. [16] Those who had seen it told the people what had happened to the demon-possessed man—and told about the pigs as well. [17] Then the people began to plead with Jesus to leave their region.

[18] As Jesus was getting into the boat, the man who had been demon-possessed begged to go with him. [19] Jesus did not let him, but said, "Go home to your family and tell them how much the Lord has done for you, and how he has had mercy on you." [20] So the man went away and began to tell in the Decapolis how much Jesus had done for him. And all the people were amazed.

Jesus Takes the Gospel to Outsiders (5:1)

The Gerasene area was in a Gentile area east of the Sea of Galilee, also known as the Sea of Tiberius. Gerasa was part of an area known as The Decapolis, a league of ten cities very much oriented to Greek culture. Some of the cities dated back to the time of Alexander the Great (fourth century B.C.), and all except Damascus were in the area of modern Jordan. The Romans tolerated the residents there, and they had as much independence as one could have in a Roman-dominated world. Along the hillsides near the seashore were many caves that served as burial spots. In ancient legends, tombs were a favorite place for demons to be found.

A key point that reinforces the thrust of the previous lesson, "Levi: Outsiders Welcome," is that Jesus went deliberately to a non-Jewish area, and the man who was healed became a witness to the life-changing power Jesus had. Matthew records that "large crowds," including people from the Decapolis area, followed Jesus (Matthew 4:25) and Mark writes about Jesus making another visit to the area later (Mark 7:31).

The Madman from Gerasa (5:2–10)

When Jesus stepped on shore in Gerasa, he met one of the most pitiful characters in the gospel story. Had the man heard of Jesus, or was it his custom to scare anyone who got out of boats? Regardless, Jesus was confronted by a man who was unbelievably strong and unrestrained. No chains or ropes could hold him. He lived a nightmare night and day; he was the epitome of a crazed person whose life was fit only for solitary confinement to graveyards and isolated places. Yet, when Jesus showed up, he recognized Jesus and ran to worship him.

What was the man's problem? We often want to impose modern ideas onto the man's situation. It may be impossible, though, for us to really know what was going on in this man from the ancient world. The reality is that Jesus met the man on the man's own turf and with the man's own understandings of systems and categories that we may never fully comprehend.

The text of Mark 5:7–10 can be confusing. Was Jesus talking to the man or to the demon(s) within the man, or both? In verse 7, the man appears to be talking, perhaps thinking that Jesus had come to Gerasa just to deal with him: *What are you going to do with me, a demonic man? Are you going to torment me, a man already tormented?* That might have been what the man was thinking. Mark notes in verse 8 that Jesus had already commanded the evil spirit to come out of the man, but it did not. Then in verse 9, Jesus asked the demon for his name. "My name is Legion," he said. The name indicates the fragmenting effect he had on the man's mind and also that more than one evil impulse was at work in the man. Then, the evil spirits began to bargain with Jesus, not wanting to be sent out of the country, and so Jesus sent them out of the man into a herd of pigs.

Whatever evil tormented the man had both identity and voice, but Jesus revealed his power over the evil forces. Jesus was continuing to reveal his identity and purpose. Mark's Gospel sees these events as part of a larger pattern that emphasizes Jesus' authority and power, including his power over nature in calming the sea (just prior to this incident, Mark 4:35–41) as well as miraculous healings, calling disciples, and other astounding actions. The events are now piling up as they reveal the nature of Jesus as God in human flesh or as Mark 1:1 states, "the Son of God."

What about the pigs? The story comes with no footnotes for sure meaning, but perhaps this was one way Jesus confirmed for the man that he was healed and would no longer be tormented. The man may have thought that whatever it was that was ruining his life was now drowned in the sea. Some might criticize the story as being cruel to animals, but the point is about what Jesus could do for such a pitiful person. Jesus restored the man's sanity and gave him a purpose. Praise God.

Understanding "demons" is complex. Some biblical accounts relating to demons cause us to think about various modern maladies. We will never solve that issue; however, one theory does provide some insight into whatever reality that troubled people in the ancient world that was explained as "demons." Diseases were explained as demons at work. *Stay*

DEMONOLOGY

Some consider demons to be the bad guys and angels the good guys. The subject is far more complex than that; however, focus your attention for a moment, not on the literalism of little devils infesting the universe but on other "demons" that often beset us. These allegorical kind of demons spread evil and cause pain. These demons may cause a person to stay immersed in grief, never really emerging from the tombs, while idolizing a special person who has died. Others have demons that lead them to addictions that plague them and destroy families. Others have demons implanted by others, memories that haunt them because of abuse by family or trusted friends. Perhaps the following demons may not appear so sinister, but they can be cancerous to our well-being: telling half-truths; being indifferent to the needs of others; believing that life is all about me; exhibiting a polite (perhaps) but negative attitude toward those who are of a different culture or race. Demonology may be a complex subject, but sometimes we provide these other demons a comfortable home in our lives. With Jesus, you can control these demons.

GOING FURTHER WITH THIS LESSON

- Study a particular mental illness that affects some person you know.

- Research the life of Dr. Wayne Oates, a Baptist pioneer in the area of pastoral care. For starters, see www.oates.org on the internet.

- Make a list of Scripture verses that relate to God's grace in good times and bad. Begin with these three: John 14:27; Romans 8:28; and Philippians 4:6–8.

- Write out what you can tell a person about your experience with Christ, how God helped you deal with a particular crisis, or how you have been especially blessed by God and/or others. Then *go and tell.*

---

away from graveyards would be the advice given to children in the first century, for demons were there. Some who understand "demons" in this way also believe that Jesus triumphed over sin and death with the cross and resurrection, and that after the resurrection "demons" were thus no longer an option in our world. Paul wrote, "Having disarmed the powers and authorities, he made a public spectacle of them, triumphing over them by the cross" (Colossians 2:15). Thus, in our world, we may exercise caution about walking around a cemetery at night, but we don't have to fear a demon taking over our bodies and tormenting us.

When Jesus Was Asked to Leave (5:14–17)

Two thousand pigs in the sea would have caused quite a commotion! People came to see, and what they saw caused them great concern. For one thing, the demoniac was clothed properly and in his right mind. Luke adds the detail that the man was "sitting at the feet of Jesus" (Luke 8:35). They had not seen that demeanor in the man for a long time, if ever. With some convoluted reasoning, the people were afraid of the man who had such a great change in his life, afraid of a man who sat at the feet of Jesus. They were accustomed to his weirdness and afraid of him, but now they were more afraid because of what Jesus had done for him. But, then they began to talk about the pigs.

Two thousand pigs represented a lot of money. That was what the people saw the most. They might have thought, *If this Jesus stays around, what else will he do to interfere with our lives?* They could not feel good about a pitiful human being healed, and they were fearful of the economic impact that Jesus might have on their area. Some never understand the value of people but get obsessed with the importance of things and money.

A Healthy Person (5:18–20)

Jesus left the area, setting sail in the boat. But just as he was doing so, the healed man begged Jesus to let him go with them. He would have made a good exhibit. But instead of showing him off, Jesus sent him off. Jesus told him to go back to his family for *show-and-tell*. He was to give the Lord credit for his change of life and the grace showed to him. Not only did the man do that, but he also went out through the Decapolis area telling what Jesus had done for him.

That is how the gospel is spread. When we have been saved or blessed, we share it with others. In a sense, the first missionary to the Decapolis area was a former demon-possessed man who had been made whole by Jesus. *Go and tell* is a frequent imperative of Scripture. We do not know all this man did after this, but whatever it was, he was a witness to what the Lord had done. Jesus healed him and gave him a purpose for the future. At that point, we all are alike. God saves us and then sends us to minister and witness.

Implications and Actions

Church people are *Converted* people, at least that's what we like to say. With the capital *C*, we have turned in faith to Jesus Christ and turned away from sin. The demon-possessed man was truly changed. Jesus changed the direction of his life, giving him peace in the present and purpose for his future. The man experienced Conversion with the big *C*.

As we go through life, many of us have need for conversion with the little *c* even if we have experienced Conversion with the big *C*.

How is that? As we grow, we become aware of areas of weakness or perhaps areas where we are symbolically chained to behaviors, attitudes, or actions that do not honor Christ, help others, or do much good within us. We may not be screaming in the darkness, but we know the darkness is there. What will we do? The truth is this: the God of the big *C* Conversion is also the god of the little *c* conversion. It is not too late for the Lord to do a *makeover* with you. If your life is out of line or warped—a little or a lot—God can do good things for you as well. You've trusted him for the big things; now trust him to fine-tune you for all that lies ahead.

QUESTIONS

1. Will you pray regularly for those who are chained to attitudes and behaviors that are disruptive and demeaning to others? Ask God how you can be an instrument of his peace.

2. How do you extend the fellowship of God's people to people who are active in your church but somehow seem not to fit in for various reasons?

3. Why do you think the swine herders and local people acted the way they did?

4. How do you answer the scriptural question of the demoniac for yourself, "What do you want with me, Jesus?" (Mark 5:6).

5. How can you implement Jesus' plan for the healed man, *Go and tell*?

FOCAL TEXT
Mark 5:22–43

BACKGROUND
Mark 5:21–43

MAIN IDEA
Both Jairus, whose daughter was dying, and the woman who was desperate to be healed relied solely on Jesus for help.

QUESTION TO EXPLORE
Where is Jesus when we need him?

STUDY AIM
To state what Jesus' help to both Jairus and the desperate woman reveal about Jesus' help with my own desperate needs

QUICK READ
Jesus met the deepest needs of two people, both of whom reached out to him, believing that Jesus could help them. Although our needs may differ from theirs, God is still able and willing to meet them.

LESSON SIX
Two Desperate People: Relying On Jesus

As a child, visiting my grandparents' home in Northeast Georgia was special. Riding Mert the mule, being around cattle and hogs, exploring in barns and buildings—what a treat for a growing boy. My grandparents had large catalogues from pioneers in the mail order business—Sears and Spiegel. My older brother and I spent many an hour looking at thousands of items. The ritual always included a large number of statements that began with, *I want this*. Although my parents did not stress over our *wants*, they stressed for our benefit the difference between *wants* and *needs*. I suppose every generation has had to learn that lesson.

Today's Scripture deals with people with great *needs*—real *needs*, not just wants. They had heard about Jesus, and they turned to him for help. They wanted help. They needed help. One family looked at Jesus as their last hope for a very sick daughter. Another woman was almost broke from seeking medical help. She was desperate to be healed. Jesus met the needs of these people, restoring their health and lives.

Jesus did not heal everyone who was sick or raise every person who died. These two incidents, though, continue to reveal Jesus as one who has unusual power and authority.

MARK 5:22–43

22 Then one of the synagogue rulers, named Jairus, came there. Seeing Jesus, he fell at his feet 23 and pleaded earnestly with him, "My little daughter is dying. Please come and put your hands on her so that she will be healed and live." 24 So Jesus went with him.

A large crowd followed and pressed around him. 25 And a woman was there who had been subject to bleeding for twelve years. 26 She had suffered a great deal under the care of many doctors and had spent all she had, yet instead of getting better she grew worse. 27 When she heard about Jesus, she came up behind him in the crowd and touched his cloak, 28 because she thought, "If I just touch his clothes, I will be healed." 29 Immediately her bleeding stopped and she felt in her body that she was freed from her suffering.

30 At once Jesus realized that power had gone out from him. He turned around in the crowd and asked, "Who touched my clothes?"

³¹ "You see the people crowding against you," his disciples answered, "and yet you can ask, 'Who touched me?'"
³² But Jesus kept looking around to see who had done it.
³³ Then the woman, knowing what had happened to her, came and fell at his feet and, trembling with fear, told him the whole truth. ³⁴ He said to her, "Daughter, your faith has healed you. Go in peace and be freed from your suffering."

³⁵ While Jesus was still speaking, some men came from the house of Jairus, the synagogue ruler. "Your daughter is dead," they said. "Why bother the teacher any more?"

³⁶ Ignoring what they said, Jesus told the synagogue ruler, "Don't be afraid; just believe."

³⁷ He did not let anyone follow him except Peter, James and John the brother of James. ³⁸ When they came to the home of the synagogue ruler, Jesus saw a commotion, with people crying and wailing loudly. ³⁹ He went in and said to them, "Why all this commotion and wailing? The child is not dead but asleep." ⁴⁰ But they laughed at him.

After he put them all out, he took the child's father and mother and the disciples who were with him, and went in where the child was. ⁴¹ He took her by the hand and said to her, *"Talitha koum!"* (which means, "Little girl, I say to you, get up!"). ⁴² Immediately the girl stood up and walked around (she was twelve years old). At this they were completely astonished. ⁴³ He gave strict orders not to let anyone know about this, and told them to give her something to eat.

Jairus's Faith in Jesus (5:22–24)

Jesus ministered to every spectrum of his society. He reached out to the tax collectors and sinners as well as having an intentional ministry among the Gentiles in the Decapolis. He also was open to Pharisees and synagogue leaders. One of these, Jairus, was a lay leader of the synagogue. He was not their priest but rather a chief administrative official. That in itself was an obstacle to overcome, for Jesus was receiving strong criticism from Jairus's colleagues. Yet, Jairus took the risk. He approached Jesus humbly and with great faith, falling submissively at the feet of Jesus.

Jairus was desperate, and so was his daughter. She was at the point of death, and Jairus believed Jesus could heal her. He pleaded with great faith, "Put your hands on her so that she will be healed and live" (Mark 5:23). You may be able to identify with the agony of a parent over a sick child. We pray and seek the best medical help. Generally, healing does come, but in this story, Jairus might have exhausted all hope in others, or he simply saw something so different in Jesus that he knew Jesus could help. Jesus went with Jairus, and so did a large crowd.

The Faith of a Desperate Woman (5:25–34)

Some of life's most interesting moments happen on our way to do something else. Have you ever had that experience? Perhaps you had your calendar all set, everything neatly arranged, but then some other need sidetracked you or you were interrupted. Although I might have been uncomfortable when those moments came, I often found that life's interruptions may provide some of the richest moments of the day. While Jesus was on the way to deal with a dying little girl, something else—someone else—caught his attention.

The crowd was large, and people jostled one another to get closer to Jesus, to hear what the master teacher was saying. A woman in the crowd risked being in Jesus' presence. She had had constant bleeding for twelve years. She was plagued by a constant flow of blood. According to Jewish law, she was ritually unclean (see Leviticus 15:25). As such, she was supposed to avoid people. If she were recognized in a group of people, her misery would have increased. She had spent a lot of time and money on doctors, but instead of being healed she was getting worse. Like Jairus, she believed Jesus had the power to heal her. She thought, "If I just touch his clothes, I will be healed" (Mark 5:28). Amazingly, when she touched just the hem of Jesus' garment, she was healed. Immediately, she felt freed from that which had plagued her so long.

Jesus could feel the energy moving out of his body. He asked, "Who touched my clothes?" (5:30). Did Jesus really not know who the person was? Although he was God in human flesh, he also was fully human.

He might not have known; however, he could also have been setting the stage for the woman to publicly confess her faith as well as be affirmed in her faith. The disciples seemed impatient with Jesus' delay. Perhaps they thought Jesus' time could be better spent with an important leader of the synagogue, but Jesus searched through the crowd for the one who touched him. An unnamed woman would not be overlooked. She needed to hear something, and so did Jesus' disciples and the crowd.

The woman had slipped back into the crowd, but now Jesus was doing the seeking. She came forward not knowing what to expect. She might have wondered whether Jesus would rebuke her for touching him. "Trembling with fear," she fell at Jesus' feet (5:33). Jesus said for her and all those listening, "Your faith has healed you" (5:34). Then Jesus blessed her with the traditional Hebrew blessing of "peace." She was healed.

Jesus helped the woman to clarify what happened. She thought that touching Jesus' clothes had brought healing, but Jesus had a different opinion. Her healing revealed Jesus' power to heal someone, but it also demonstrated the value of faith, "Your faith has healed you" (5:34). Faith, however, is not just talk or feeling. Faith also includes actions (see James 1:22). After she heard about Jesus, she sought Jesus. She believed Jesus could make her well. She put herself into position to be healed, and she did all she knew how to do to make it possible, even reaching out to touch Jesus' clothing. These are all aspects of faith.

Do not underestimate the importance of putting yourself into position for God to bless you. That can be done in many traditional ways, such as going to church, having a consistent devotional time with God each day, or staying obedient to God's will. By staying faithful and seeking God's presence, you have made a big step in actually experiencing grace and blessing. The woman's touch was not an act of *press the magic button and all will be well*, but it was a part of the process that led her to wholeness. Her faith and trust in Jesus was the key. Jesus freed her from her long time of emotional and physical distress. She now had healing and peace.

What About Jairus's Daughter? (5:35–43)

Jesus was on the way to see Jairus's daughter when he stopped to deal with the woman. During that experience, word came from Jairus's house that his daughter had died. The bearer of bad news told Jairus not to trouble Jesus any longer, for it was too late. But Jesus had a better word for Jairus: "Don't be afraid; just believe" (Mark 5:36). The disciples had heard Jesus talk about fear and faith before, for that was Jesus' message when they were scared to death in a storm on the Sea of Galilee (4:35–41). At that time they asked, "Who is this? Even the wind and sea obey him!" (4:41) The disciples were not only hearing answers to their questions as they walked with Jesus, but they also were seeing the answers.

Jesus took only three of the disciples with him to Jairus's house. They represented what appears to have been the inner circle of leadership among the disciples. The mourners had already gathered, and they scoffed at Jesus' suggestion that the girl was not dead. Jesus sent them all outside and took her father and mother along with the disciples into the room.

Jesus took the girl's hand and said, "Get up!" (5:41). The girl immediately "stood up and walked around" (5:42), and those present were

NO MORE MOURNING

Mourning was extensive in first-century Judaism. When death came, the focus was on the finality of death. Loud wailing began and continued to the grave. People tore their clothes as a symbol of a broken heart and wore these torn clothes for a month or so. Mourners practiced restraint on food, clothing, and many different activities.

Some mourners were professionals, amplifying the mourning of the relatives. Perhaps these mourners had already gathered for Jairus's daughter. The burial followed death as soon as possible, usually within twenty-four hours, but the mourning continued at varying lengths.

The New Testament faith gave new meaning to mourning customs. Christian hope permeated the mourning atmosphere, recognizing Jesus' victory over sin and death. In the Book of Revelation, the picture of heaven is a wonderful place where there will be no more mourning or sorrow, for we will be in God's presence forever (Revelation 21:1–4). Christians mourn on earth, but as Paul wrote, we do not "grieve like the rest of men, who have no hope" (1 Thess. 4:13).

astonished. Then Jesus instructed the parents not to tell anyone about what had happened. People eventually would know what happened, but Jesus did not want to attract more mere *thrill seekers*. Jesus also told the parents to give their little girl something to eat. Jesus met the needs of the parents and the child, and now the parents needed to assume responsibility for her care. Jesus was asked to help, and he did. His power over disease and death continued to add to the disciples' understanding of who Jesus was.

A key ingredient in the girl's restoration was the faith of her father in seeking Jesus' help. The faith of Jairus and that of the woman with the plague of constant bleeding were similar. They both believed that Jesus was the answer to their deepest desires and needs. Jairus said nothing about Jesus' delay when he healed the woman. Having seen Jesus deal with her, Jairus readily accepted Jesus' word, "Don't be afraid; just believe" (5:36). Probably in grief but still believing, Jairus had the blessed experience of Jesus walking with him every step of the way to his home. That's the way God is when any believer goes through difficult times.

Was the girl dead? Everyone present thought she was dead, but Jesus' statement may not be clear to us because the word here translated "asleep" is often used to describe *death* (see 1 Thessalonians 5:10; see also John 11:11–14). Did Jesus mean that the little girl was dead or that she was in what we might call a coma? Could Jesus' words mean, *She may appear dead to you, but I can bring a person out of a deep sleep (coma) or even raise them from the dead*? Whatever our understanding—and Jesus is fully capable of both—those present knew that Jesus did something for the girl that restored her health and life. That is what Jairus believed Jesus could do. (See also Luke 8:55, "Her spirit returned. . . .")

Incorporating Truth Into Our Lives

We pray for people to be healed. That is good and right; intercessory prayer is an important part of what we can do as Christians (see 1 Samuel 12:23). God is still in the business of healing and health, but God has so many more resources to use today than he did 2,000 years ago. I believe very strongly in the relationship of faith and healing, but I am suspicious of those who claim to be faith healers. The whole subject of prayer, suffering, and healing is complex and defies simple answers. One thing

FAITH AND HEALING

A faithful church member was affected by severe arthritis for many years. She tried everything she knew—doctors, specialists, many medicines and herbal treatments. However, her condition became almost unbearable. She decided to attend a faith healing service. She was prayed over and pronounced healed, but she was not. Growing frustrated, she asked the healer why she was not better. He said, *You did not have enough faith.*

She went home, wondering whether it really was her fault. The next morning, she said to you, *Help me. I have faith, but what went wrong?* What would you say to her?

that helps us keep perspective is that as far as we know, all of those who received a miracle of restored health by Jesus eventually died.

The miracles of Jesus encourage us to turn all our concerns and cares over to Jesus. Pray for healing, for God hears and always answers our prayers. Sometimes we get the temporary miracle of restored health, what seems to be a *yes* to our prayer. God's answer may also appear to be *no*. We do not know all the *whys* of prayer, sickness, and death, but in reality, God's *no* answer may be, *Wait, I will take care of all things my own way, either within time or in heaven itself.*

In all times and circumstances, however, we get the miracle of grace (see 2 Corinthians 12:9). God will give us grace and strength to deal with whatever we or our loved ones face, and we know that even the coroner's verdict of death is not the final answer. For the Christian, death becomes the doorway to a fuller experience with God, and in some sense, death becomes God's perfect healing as we are taken to be with God forever (see John 14:1–3). Whatever happens with our prayer request, God never leaves us alone and always acts for our good.

Our role is to continue to trust. Our faith will not force God to act, but genuine faith helps us to deal with life, live more effectively, and put ourselves in position for God to work all things together for our good (see Romans 8:28). Whatever dilemma or difficulty we face, especially when the circumstances may even seem desperate, we do not deal with life's tough issues alone. God is with us and will see us through.

QUESTIONS

1. How does your faith compare to that of Jairus?

2. After some bad experience, why do people ask, *Why me?* Should they ask, *Why not me?*

3. What do you need to change so you can put yourself into position for God to use or bless your life?

4. How can you be part of the answer to someone's prayer or need? Have you asked God?

5. Are you willing, as Jairus and the unnamed woman were, to ask Jesus to meet your needs and trust him for the results?

FOCAL TEXT
Mark 6:1–6

BACKGROUND
Mark 6:1–6

MAIN IDEA
People from Jesus' hometown failed to express faith in Jesus and receive his blessings because they were unwilling to see him for who he truly was.

QUESTION TO EXPLORE
In what ways are you stuck in the ordinary when faith is challenging you to go further?

STUDY AIM
To identify and decide to overcome barriers to my fully exercising faith in Jesus

QUICK READ
"Familiarity breeds contempt," we've heard. Can familiarity also breed faithlessness? That is what was at stake as Jesus visited his hometown.

LESSON SEVEN
Hometown People: Stuck in the Ordinary

Sometimes familiarity is good. Whether it's in church, in the car, or on our smart phone, we may well enjoy listening to the same songs over and over. Couples sleep on their same sides of the bed for an entire marriage and may feel uncomfortable when they have to swap sides. Children watch the same movies over and over until grown-ups think their ears will bleed if they hear it one more time. If only you could taste your mom's (insert your favorite meal here) just one more time.

A certain comfort comes to us when things are familiar. When the familiar gets rearranged, we are confronted with grief, whether minor or major, over the changes in our lives. In the story for this lesson, familiarity plays a major role. The people of Nazareth were familiar with the hometown boy named Jesus. But as this passage unfolds, we learn that their familiarity with the boy Jesus made them very uncomfortable with the adult Jesus, in whom they failed to see the power of God at work.[1]

MARK 6:1–6

[1] He left that place and came to his hometown, and his disciples followed him. [2] On the sabbath he began to teach in the synagogue, and many who heard him were astounded. They said, "Where did this man get all this? What is this wisdom that has been given to him? What deeds of power are being done by his hands! [3] Is not this the carpenter, the son of Mary and brother of James and Joses and Judas and Simon, and are not his sisters here with us?" And they took offense at him. [4] Then Jesus said to them, "Prophets are not without honor, except in their hometown, and among their own kin, and in their own house." [5] And he could do no deed of power there, except that he laid his hands on a few sick people and cured them. 6 And he was amazed at their unbelief.

Astounded in the Synagogue (6:1–2a)

Jesus came to his hometown with his disciples in tow. Mark 1:9 and 1:24 tell us that we're talking about Nazareth, a small town in the region of Galilee. Back in Mark 5 Jesus performed three miracles that demonstrated his power to the people around him. In particular, in Mark 5, studied in lesson six, Jairus and the woman with the hemorrhage came to Jesus because they'd heard about his power and believed he could make a difference in their lives. They came with faith in place already. However, when Jesus got to his hometown, the story changed. There Jesus encountered people who lacked faith. By the end of his time with them they would also lack the miracles they sought as proof of Jesus' power.

A mean-spirited group of people met Jesus in Nazareth. They come across as though mocking Jesus in this passage, and their behavior was certainly not flattering to them or to the Messiah. We might imagine that they expected to encounter the Jesus they had known all along, but instead a very different person confronted them.

On the first Sabbath after his return, Jesus and the disciples went to the synagogue. There Jesus began teaching, and many "were astounded." But this wasn't the kind of astonishment sensed by others who heard Jesus' teaching. In fact, their astonishment was more skeptical than anything else, as we shall see in the next verses.

Incredulous Questions (6:2b–4)

Verses 2b–3 contain several questions the crowd asked after they heard Jesus teach. From this passage, we don't know exactly what Jesus taught that day, but clearly Jesus taught something that drove the people to question the source of his power and authority. Likely, it angered them in some way. Their questions are surprising.

The questions are surprising not because of what they asked, but because of who was asking. These people asking were the very same people who had known Jesus from his childhood and youth and into adulthood. They already knew the answers to their own questions. These questions did not seek information or insight but rather were barbs intended to express antagonism.

One possible reason for their questioning is that they knew Jesus to be the son of a carpenter and a tradesman himself. He likely would not have been formally educated in his social class. Thus his teaching and authority would have caused quite a stir, reminiscent of families today who send a child off to college for the first time in the family history. The returning *enlightened* student may well stand the chance of being regarded as *uppity* or as one who has left the family behind intellectually. This is a possible source for the people's disdain. They sensed that Jesus had grown and changed and was somehow different. Yet they did not grasp that Jesus' differentness was the in-breaking of God and a revealing of God in human flesh.

First question, "Where did this man get all this?"

Likely Jesus was offering commentary on the Hebrew Scripture, or offering interpretations like a rabbi would give to provide guidance for life. Perhaps the question was asked with admiration for his knowledge, but in reality the tone of the people was incredulous. They expected to see the Jesus they had always known around town, but here he was very different from them even though he was one of them. This ordinary man had turned into a wise teacher, but they didn't trust his words because they knew his background.

Second question, "What is this wisdom that has been given to him?"

This question makes it obvious that no matter what Jesus had said, the people labeled it "wisdom." Even though a carpenter was a craftsman, being a carpenter was still an humble occupation. What Jesus said and what they knew about him didn't fit, in their minds.

Jesus' training with a chisel didn't likely prepare him to be a teacher and healer, and yet Mark seems to play on this when he recorded, "What deeds of power are being done by his hands!" (Mark 6:2). Jesus healed with his hands, the very same hands that planed beams. The healing hands were likely as roughly hewn as the raw materials with which Jesus worked. Yet healing had come by these very hands. Too, we understand in retrospect how those hands, once nail-pierced for humanity's sin, would become a perpetual well-spring of healing for people across all time.

Question three, "Is not this the carpenter, the son of Mary and brother of James and Joses and Judas and Simon, and are not his sisters here with us?"

The final question sounds like a leading question for some juicy gossip. The townspeople identified his family, but they did so without the traditional *bar Joseph*—son of Joseph—lineage marker we would expect from Jewish culture. Instead of naming Jesus as the son of Joseph, they associated him only with Mary and his siblings. Consider several potential readings on this:

1. First, it could have been an insult to Jesus' parentage. Imagine the thinking as, *Well, we really don't know who his father was, and so this wisdom could come from that side of the family.*

2. Or another reading is that it was an insult to Jesus' role as the oldest child of widowed Mary. Imagine that thinking as, *If he really cared about his mother and family, he would be home tending to his occupation as a carpenter and caring for his family.*

3. A third reading is that by identifying Jesus with those siblings the townspeople were in effect saying there was no way Jesus could be a successful preacher or prophet with the family he had. Imagine that thinking as, *Oh, you know those children of Mary's. That is one trashy family. I just don't see how anything good could come from them!*

What "Stuck" Looks Like (6:5–6)

Verse 5 begins, " . . . He could do no deed of power there. . . ." In essence, Jesus was rendered powerless. This seems incongruent with the power of God. Surely God is able to do whatever God chooses to do, even when in

No Halo Here

The townsfolk were negative about Jesus, but there is a silver lining for us in their cloudy disposition: Jesus came across as an ordinary person. Yes, he had a history of miracles, healings, and profound teaching. But to the people who knew him, he was just another human being like them. He had no halo, no holy glow as some paintings portray Jesus to have.

This benefits Christians, making it easier to see that God really did become human, in the flesh, and to know what it is like to be tempted, weak, happy, sad, abandoned, befriended, loved, and despised. Consider Paul's word in 2 Corinthians 8:9, "For you know the generous act of our Lord Jesus Christ, that though he was rich, yet for your sakes he became poor, so that by his poverty you might become rich." That Jesus came in this manner and without a halo is an encouraging word.

the human form of Jesus! Yet here we are confronted with the powerlessness of Jesus due to the lack of belief.

The easy answer to this conundrum would be that logic often appealed to by the *gospel of prosperity* theology that proclaims, *If you believe it hard enough and are just faithful enough, then God will give you a miracle.* If we apply that logic to this passage the answer would be: *If the people of Nazareth had only believed enough, then Jesus would have been able to do more than a few simple healings.*

But that answer falls short. Instead, a more nuanced approach is to understand that Jesus is responsive to people who are responsive to him.

CHECKPOINTS OF FRESH FAITH

Avoid the pitfalls of familiarity by implementing these practical tips to keep your faith fresh:

- Read familiar passages of Scripture carefully, looking for ideas, words, or phrases that are new to you.
- Change where and how you pray. If you pray silently, pray aloud. If you pray aloud, try praying silently.
- Memorize a new passage of Scripture.
- Take a prayer walk somewhere different each week.
- Learn the tune and the words to an unfamiliar hymn or Christian song.
- Ask an old friend to tell you what's going on in his or her spiritual life. Really listen.
- Pray with someone else, aloud, so you can hear each other pray.
- Read a classic Christian book you've never read. Try *Pilgrim's Progress, Desiring God, The Ragamuffin Gospel, Treatise on the Love of God,* or almost anything by C.S. Lewis. Some of these are free on the Internet.
- Go on a silent retreat.
- Fast for 24 hours.

The problem of powerlessness in this story tells us less about the Father or the Son than it tells us about humanity. It reveals the interrelatedness of God and humans in this world, and it hints at the possibility that God wants us to join with him in the miraculous nature of the gospel. The powerlessness of Jesus in this situation is not just an incident pointing to the humanity of Jesus. Rather, it is an event that reveals nothing less than the very nature of how God works in the world: in partnership with people.

The passage moves from the astonishment of the people to the amazement of Jesus at their lack of belief. Because of the people's lack of faith, Jesus could do no miracles. Perhaps their faith lacked because they knew Jesus as a boy, but more realistically their faith lagged because they were hung up on their old view of Jesus and unwilling and unable to see him as the Son of God.

In short, these people were stuck! They were stuck in the familiar, they were stuck in a rut. They were stuck by their lifetime of assumptions, as well as by an unwillingness to see anything or anyone differently than their self-constructed perceptions allowed. What opportunities had they already missed in life before Jesus' return to his hometown? What blessings had they missed because of an unwillingness to look with fresh eyes on a familiar figure?

Implications and Actions

Have we today, like those of Nazareth so long ago, grown too familiar with Jesus? It is easy to discredit the townspeople of that day because of their dismissiveness of Jesus, but let's conduct some self-examination lest we commit the same sin.

It is tempting to gloss over this passage with a smug charge of faithlessness and miss the larger point that Jesus beckons us constantly to explore new frontiers of faith. We do this by engaging in worship and study with our faith community, but also through mission and service to our surrounding community. We too are called into participation with God in the reconciliation of the world.

QUESTIONS

1. This encounter suggests that Jesus appeared to the people as an ordinary man. Does God appear in ordinary ways still today? Do you have ways of identifying God in the world around you? What are those ways?

2. The people "took offense" at Jesus (Mark 6:3). In what ways does your church take offense to the teachings of Jesus? In what ways do *you* take offense?

3. In what way(s) is your own life stuck as the townspeople of Nazareth were stuck? Does your faith need some proof from God for a boost? Are you skeptical that the power of God is at work in the world today?

4. What would it take to convince you that Jesus is the Son of God? The story from the Bible? The words of a song or sermon? The testimony of someone you know? Something else?

5. Mark 6:5 tells us that Jesus could not do any miracles except to heal a few people, suggesting that his power was linked to the people's unbelief. Is God's power in our lives limited by our lack of faith? If so, how? In what ways is God's power limited by your own lack of faith?

NOTES

1. Unless otherwise indicated, all Scripture quotations on the back cover, in "Introducing The Gospel of Mark: People Responding to Jesus," in lessons 7—9, 12–13, and in the Christmas lesson are taken from the New Revised Standard Version Bible.

MAIN IDEA

The religious leaders needed the radically free approach of Jesus to true relationship with God, for their carefully keeping their traditions wasn't working.

QUESTION TO EXPLORE

What traditions keep us from entering and living fully in a relationship with God?

STUDY AIM

To summarize Jesus' teachings on relating to God and to evaluate whether my life before God is based on outward tradition or genuine relationship

QUICK READ

Jesus challenged the Pharisees' traditions and taught that actions of goodness that spring from a heart right with God are what is important, not keeping religious rituals and traditions.

LESSON EIGHT
The Religious Leaders: Bound By Tradition

The story has been told and retold countless times, but consider it once more. A newlywed wife is preparing a ham, and she cuts off the end of the ham before putting it in the roaster. The new husband looks on with curiosity and asks, "Why did you cut the end off the ham?"

"Because that's how it's done."

"But why?" he asks.

"Well, that's how my mother always cooked it."

So the young man calls his mother-in-law on the phone to ask about this. Her answer was the same as her daughter's, "That's just how you do it. That's how my mother always cooked it."

Intrigued and determined to get to the root cause, he called the grandmother and queried her the same way. The answer? She had a small oven, and the ham wouldn't fit without cutting off the end. She had a real reason for doing that, but her daughter and granddaughter simply did it because *that's the way we do it in our family*. They blindly followed custom. Which leads us to ask how many customs and rituals do we follow blindly but for which there is no good reason to continue?

As we approach Mark 7:1–23, we'll be asking questions about our religious practices with an eye on Jesus to give us insight to evaluate whether our relationship with God is based on outward tradition or true relationship.

MARK 7:1–23

¹ Now when the Pharisees and some of the scribes who had come from Jerusalem gathered around him, ² they noticed that some of his disciples were eating with defiled hands, that is, without washing them. ³ (For the Pharisees, and all the Jews, do not eat unless they thoroughly wash their hands, thus observing the tradition of the elders; ⁴ and they do not eat anything from the market unless they wash it; and there are also many other traditions that they observe, the washing of cups, pots, and bronze kettles.) ⁵ So the Pharisees and the scribes asked him, "Why do your disciples not live according to the tradition of the elders, but eat with defiled hands?"

⁶ He said to them, "Isaiah prophesied rightly about you hypocrites, as it is written,

'This people honors me with their lips,
but their hearts are far from me;
⁷ in vain do they worship me,
teaching human precepts as doctrines.'

⁸ You abandon the commandment of God and hold to human tradition."

⁹ Then he said to them, "You have a fine way of rejecting the commandment of God in order to keep your tradition! ¹⁰ For Moses said, 'Honor your father and your mother'; and, 'Whoever speaks evil of father or mother must surely die.' ¹¹ But you say that if anyone tells father or mother, 'Whatever support you might have had from me is Corban' (that is, an offering to God) — ¹² then you no longer permit doing anything for a father or mother, ¹³ thus making void the word of God through your tradition that you have handed on. And you do many things like this."

¹⁴ Then he called the crowd again and said to them, "Listen to me, all of you, and understand: ¹⁵ there is nothing outside a person that by going in can defile, but the things that come out are what defile."

¹⁷ When he had left the crowd and entered the house, his disciples asked him about the parable. ¹⁸ He said to them, "Then do you also fail to understand? Do you not see that whatever goes into a person from outside cannot defile, ¹⁹ since it enters, not the heart but the stomach, and goes out into the sewer?" (Thus he declared all foods clean.) ²⁰ And he said, "It is what comes out of a person that defiles. ²¹ For it is from within, from the human heart, that evil intentions come: fornication, theft, murder, ²² adultery, avarice, wickedness, deceit, licentiousness, envy, slander, pride, folly. ²³ All these evil things come from within, and they defile a person."

Rituals of the Pharisees (7:1–5)

Mark 6:7–56, prior to this passage in Mark 7 and after the passage studied in lesson seven (Mark 6:1–6), includes the following events: John the Baptist being executed; Jesus feeding the five thousand; and Jesus displaying his power in a walk on the water. Lesson nine will return to study Mark 6:45–52 in a lesson about how the disciples were slow to understand what Jesus was about. So lesson eight focuses on the traditions that fettered the religious leaders of Jesus' day.

These Pharisees had many rituals to follow as a part of their religious practice. They were renowned for excellence at keeping the law, but Jesus criticized them for putting the rituals above the purposes the rituals aimed to maintain. In some ways it is easy to criticize or condemn these religiously strict people. Hypocrisy is the word that aptly describes their faith. However, they were earnestly pursuing their religion. Many of us, like them, crave order and stability to help us feel secure. It is likely that their rituals, based in law, organized the community and made life orderly for many people.

In addition, these rituals helped the Jewish people maintain an identity as God's chosen people in a time when, one after another, foreign governments ruled Israel. Lest the people be tempted to convert to the pantheon of gods of their conquerors, many of the Pharisees likely clung to the purification rituals as a way of maintaining loyalty to God, the God of the Exodus and the return from Exile.

So while the traditions of the Pharisees and other Jews were not necessarily bad, something went wrong along the way. Something happened that moved the Pharisees to the place where the tradition was more important than the God whom the tradition was meant to honor.

Mark used an aside to address his audience in verses 3–4. This aside tells a bit about Mark's purpose and his background. First it tells us Mark was writing to an audience who would need some explanation about Jewish rituals of purification. This is a sign that the early church at the time of Mark's writing had begun to expand to Gentiles. They would not have known about these particular rituals, and an explanation would have set the context for them. This is one feature that makes Mark's Gospel accessible to new Christians.

Second, this aside indicates that Mark was bringing us in on the inner meaning of this encounter. He was setting us up for the second half of

A CASE STUDY ON CRYING BABIES, HATS, AND MARBLES IN WORSHIP

Once upon a time there was a church where worship was always being disrupted. A screaming baby with a wet bottom shattered the quiet, peaceful worship service one Sunday.

The next Sunday the congregation was disturbed because a teen-age boy wore a hat to church. Everyone knew he had never come to church before and he was there only because of a cute girl who'd invited him.

The third Sunday of the month a child near the back of the auditorium dropped a bag of marbles during the sermon. Each marble rolled loudly down the sloped hardwood floors, disrupting the pastor's very important sermon.

Something similar happened every Sunday for six weeks until one day a deacon, not known for his smiling radiance, stood up to address the business meeting about distractions in worship.

What do you think he said? What should he have said?

the passage (beginning at 7:14), so that when Jesus' disciples asked Jesus about the meaning of the parable, we will be examining whether we ourselves understand, too. More importantly, bringing us in on the traditions of purity law will help us see and distinguish between what is God's command and what is a merely human tradition or ritual.

Not seeing this distinction clearly, the Pharisees were prompted to ask Jesus why he and his disciples didn't follow the traditions of the elders. To answer, Jesus turned to the prophetic tradition and to the *Torah* (law).

Jesus Responds with an Appeal to the Prophets (7:6–8)

Invoking the writing of the prophet Isaiah, Jesus delivered a not-so-subtle charge of hypocrisy. Jesus quoted a passage from Isaiah 29:11 that flies in the face of empty ritual and claims God's favor for those who honor God with their hearts, not with their lips and empty human traditions. The rituals of purification had become a means of judging other people.

OUTWARD TRADITION OR GENUINE RELATIONSHIP WITH GOD?

Score the following statements OT or GR.

_____ 1. A man is late for Sunday School because he bought breakfast for a homeless man on the street.

_____ 2. A person goes to church every Sunday but is engaged in an extramarital affair.

_____ 3. A teenager tithes on his income from a summer job.

_____ 4. A woman sings in the church choir every Sunday with joy but doesn't agree with everything her church teaches.

_____ 5. The Kitchen Committee chair keeps the kitchen spotless but gets agitated when non-church members rent the kitchen and fail to clean it to his standards.

_____ 6. A youth leader asks a teen not to return to church because the teen expresses views that are quite different from the church's views and practices.

Jesus appealed to the prophetic tradition of Isaiah to show the Pharisees that their human tradition would have to take a back seat to the guidance offered by the prophets. Moreover, it illustrated that Jesus was more interested in what the spirit of the law was doing to help people be in relationship to God than he was in how the letter of the law might keep a person purified of sin.

Substitution of Human Tradition for God's Commandments (7:9–13)

Jesus moved on to blast the Pharisees for "rejecting the commandment of God in order to keep your tradition!" (Mark 7:9). He pointed out how Moses commanded honor for father and mother. Then he charged the Pharisees with using the religious ritual of Corban as an excuse for giving no more support to an aging parent.

"Corban" was a word from Hebrew that simply meant *an offering or vow to God*. The Pharisees would earmark money or sacrifices for this offering, and the offering then could not be used for the care of their elderly parents. Jesus condemned this practice and illustrated again how the Pharisees had elevated human tradition above the commands of God.

Listen and Understand (7:14–23)

As we move to Mark 7:14, we note that the gathering around Jesus has changed. Jesus focused his attention on the observers who were standing nearby ("the crowd"). To clarify his point in the previous verses, Jesus explained that it is not the things that go into a person that defile, but rather the things that come out of a person that make the person unclean.

Verse 17 marks another change in audience. Jesus "had left the crowd and entered the house" and was with only his disciples. They were asking about the whole of the conversation because they didn't understand everything. Clearly what Jesus was saying to them was new material they weren't grasping. Jesus replied to them, "Do you also fail to understand?" (7:18). Would you have understood?

The disciples were perplexed because Jesus was clarifying what is important to God, but what Jesus was saying opposed the basic religious practices and beliefs of the day. What Jesus said would be as unsettling to Christians today if challenged about some of our comfortable religious practices that are human instituted.

In verse 19, Mark gave another aside to his audience, stating that thus Jesus "declared all foods clean." A careful consideration reveals that Jesus did not himself say that all foods were to be ritually clean, but that was what Mark interpreted him to mean. The literal Greek states *cleansing all foods*, not "Thus he declared all foods clean." This statement invites the reader to enter into the task of careful discernment of what truly is good for a person—not just in diet—who is following the path of faith in Jesus.

In order to relate to God in authentic ways, Christians are called to consider whether their life before God is based on outward tradition or genuine relationship. Jesus clearly differentiated between commandments of God and practices that are devised by human beings. He also distinguished between the words of the prophets and the practices of the Pharisees.

Implications and Actions

We may reject the Pharisees' attitudes and practices, but we are not above the misdeeds that emerge from the human heart. We are all capable of "fornication, theft, murder, adultery, avarice, wickedness, deceit, licentiousness, envy, slander, pride, folly" (7:21b–22). We live as the Pharisees did when we insist that we and others honor religious practices that are not mandated by God's commands in Scripture.

It is important, then, that we routinely review our own lives for hypocrisy. The familiar things of our faith can be the very things that are keeping us from having a radically free and true relationship with God.

It is equally important that congregations review their activities to reject empty rituals, unfruitful practices, and traditions that are not rooted in Scripture. *We've always done it that way before* are perhaps the most dangerous words used in the church to preserve the status quo.

QUESTIONS

1. Which is easier, following a prescribed religious ritual or living a life faithful to the way of Jesus? Why? What makes one way harder than the other?

2. What things get under your skin about your church? If you really stop to think about those things, how many of them are superficial? How many are really in violation of what it means to be a faithful follower of Jesus?

3. Jesus used the word "heart" or "hearts" three times in this passage (Mark 7:6, 19, 21) in describing how we should relate to God. What does Jesus' use of the word "heart" suggest to you?

4. What attitudes and actions in your life need improvement in order for you to connect more closely to God? Where do you find support and accountability to make the necessary changes?

5. What rituals and customs of your church make you comfortable or uncomfortable?

FOCAL TEXT
Mark 6:45–52; 8:1–21

BACKGROUND
Mark 4:35–41; 6:6b–13,
30–52; 8:1–21

MAIN IDEA

In spite of the many ways in which Jesus demonstrated who he was, the disciples were slow to understand.

QUESTIONS TO EXPLORE

Why do we not yet understand who Jesus is? How can we?

STUDY AIM

To trace the events in which the disciples were slow to understand Jesus' identity and to analyze how I myself fail to understand who Jesus is

QUICK READ

The disciples saw Jesus walking on the water and were present when he fed thousands of people. They had seen him perform other miracles. Yet they still failed to understand who Jesus was.

LESSON NINE
The Disciples: Slow to Get It

Kids love "Where's Waldo" books and games. Waldo is a cartoon character dressed in his red- and white-striped rugby shirt. He hides in plain sight waiting to be discovered in pictures, videos, and books. It takes a keen eye and attention to detail, but with enough time and focus you can always find Waldo in the scene. Usually when you find him, there is a *duh* moment because of how plainly he is visible, and yet it takes effort to find him.

Perhaps that's a good metaphor for the disciples' understanding of Jesus. In our view, Jesus' power may be right in plain sight, but to the disciples it seemed elusive. With our 2,000 years of history and an understanding of the cross and resurrection, our view is better. Undoubtedly, these disciples were *slow to get it*, but are we really much different? Let's dive into the passages as a way of examining ourselves in this light.

Deeper understanding of the focal passage begins by setting the events in their larger context. Mark 6 includes the sending of the disciples two by two into the surrounding communities (Mark 6:6b–13). Jesus gave them authority over evil spirits, and they went forth preaching repentance, casting out demons, and healing the sick. They were successful in the mission, and yet still they lacked understanding of Jesus and the power of Jesus within them.

This lack of understanding is obvious a few scenes later when they witnessed and were party to the feeding of the 5,000 (6:30–44). Jesus encouraged them to solve the problem of the hungry crowd, "You give them something to eat" (6:37). He knew they had the power to solve the problem, but they still didn't sense it. We should be aware of their lack of understanding in each of these scenes because these scenes set the stage to gain insight into our focal passage.

MARK 6:45–52

45 Immediately he made his disciples get into the boat and go on ahead to the other side, to Bethsaida, while he dismissed the crowd. 46 After saying farewell to them, he went up on the mountain to pray.

47 When evening came, the boat was out on the sea, and he was alone on the land. 48 When he saw that they were straining

at the oars against an adverse wind, he came towards them early in the morning, walking on the sea. He intended to pass them by. [49] But when they saw him walking on the sea, they thought it was a ghost and cried out; [50] for they all saw him and were terrified. But immediately he spoke to them and said, "Take heart, it is I; do not be afraid." [51] Then he got into the boat with them and the wind ceased. And they were utterly astounded, [52] for they did not understand about the loaves, but their hearts were hardened.

MARK 8:1–21

[1] In those days when there was again a great crowd without anything to eat, he called his disciples and said to them, [2] "I have compassion for the crowd, because they have been with me now for three days and have nothing to eat. [3] If I send them away hungry to their homes, they will faint on the way—and some of them have come from a great distance." [4] His disciples replied, "How can one feed these people with bread here in the desert?" [5] He asked them, "How many loaves do you have?" They said, "Seven." [6] Then he ordered the crowd to sit down on the ground; and he took the seven loaves, and after giving thanks he broke them and gave them to his disciples to distribute; and they distributed them to the crowd. [7] They had also a few small fish; and after blessing them, he ordered that these too should be distributed. [8] They ate and were filled; and they took up the broken pieces left over, seven baskets full. [9] Now there were about four thousand people. And he sent them away. [10] And immediately he got into the boat with his disciples and went to the district of Dalmanutha.

[11] The Pharisees came and began to argue with him, asking him for a sign from heaven, to test him. [12] And he sighed deeply in his spirit and said, "Why does this generation ask for a sign? Truly I tell you, no sign will be given to this generation." [13] And he left them, and getting into the boat again, he went across to the other side.

[14] Now the disciples had forgotten to bring any bread; and they had only one loaf with them in the boat. [15] And he cautioned them,

saying, "Watch out—beware of the yeast of the Pharisees and the yeast of Herod." [16] They said to one another, "It is because we have no bread." [17] And becoming aware of it, Jesus said to them, "Why are you talking about having no bread? Do you still not perceive or understand? Are your hearts hardened? [18] Do you have eyes, and fail to see? Do you have ears, and fail to hear? And do you not remember? [19] When I broke the five loaves for the five thousand, how many baskets full of broken pieces did you collect?" They said to him, "Twelve." [20] "And the seven for the four thousand, how many baskets full of broken pieces did you collect?" And they said to him, "Seven." [21] Then he said to them, "Do you not yet understand?"

Did Jesus Just Walk By on the Water? (6:45–52)

After Jesus' time with the crowd he fed, he sent the disciples ahead of him in a boat to Bethsaida. He took some time to go and pray on the mountainside. It was there in the evening that he saw the disciples straining to row the boat against a very hard wind. (The Greek reads, *about the fourth watch of the night*, which was between 3 a.m. and 6 a.m.)

Jesus was walking on the water within sight of the boat, and the disciples thought they were seeing "a ghost" (6:49). What they saw terrified them, and they remained in fear until Jesus was in the boat with them and the storm had calmed.

Verse 51 states that "they were utterly astounded" because they didn't understand the miracle of the feeding of the 5,000 and, what's more, "their hearts were hardened." They still did not understand who Jesus was or what he was about.

These disciples had now seen several events that *should* have convinced them of the special nature of Jesus and helped them to see the reign of God breaking into their world. Yet somehow they'd missed it again. They had seen Jesus feed a crowd of 5,000 men with five loaves and two fish, but they hadn't gotten the meaning of the event. The healings hadn't done the trick either. Further, seeing Jesus walk on the water in the midst of the high winds and waves didn't do it. If the disciples who were there and saw all this with their own eyes were this slow to get it, should we be surprised that it takes us so long to *get* what Jesus is doing in our own lives?

Reflect on lesson seven on Mark 6 about the hometown folks' failure to understand Jesus. Then consider lesson eight on Mark 7 and compare the Pharisees who didn't *get it* with these disciples' inability to *get it*. It's not hard to conclude that literally *everyone* around Jesus saw but didn't understand. What frustration Jesus must have felt with the people around him!

4,000 for Dinner—What to Serve? (8:1–10)

There is some debate about whether this feeding in Mark 8:1–10 is the same as the one in Mark 6:30–44. However, there is also the suggestion that the first feeding was among the Jews and this one in Mark 8:1–10 is among the Gentiles. As support for this view, note that in 7:24–30 there is an exchange between Jesus and the Syrophoenician woman. She begged Jesus for a miracle, arguing that even the dogs got crumbs from the table. Even though she was not Jewish, she was convinced that just a scrap of Jesus' power would be more than enough for her need. Oddly, the only ones who seemed to *get it* about Jesus were the ones who would have been least expected to understand. Set against that story, it is probable that Mark was offering this second feeding story as pointing to some really *big crumbs* for the Gentiles.

With regard to the audience, we should focus on these dense disciples. This time Jesus had been teaching for three days (8:2), and he called the disciples to him to suggest they do something about the physical nourishment of the people. Once again the disciples issued a collective *duh* when they said, "How can one feed these people with bread here in the desert?" (8:4).

Once again Jesus took leadership and used miraculous powers to feed the people. The meal was abundant, and there were leftovers. Some features are similar and others are different between the two feeding narratives (see 6:30–44). The one common theme is that, once again, the disciples were slow to *get it*. We are invited again to reflect on why these disciples were so slow to see and understand and to ask the question of

BOATS IN THE BIBLE

Two scenes in this lesson involve boats. In one scene Jesus walked on the water up to the boat containing the disciples rowing hard against the wind (Mark 6:47–52). In another Jesus was in a boat with one loaf of bread and a boatload of dense disciples (8:14).

Boats figure prominently in the Bible, and especially in Mark's Gospel. Boats were a mainstay of commerce and transportation. Fishing supported the food supply, and boats also served to move people quickly to their destinations.

- Jonah was thrown off a boat (Jonah 1:3).
- Noah built a really big boat for eight people and the animals (Genesis 7:15–19).
- Paul spent lots of time on a boat (Acts 20:13, for one example).
- Jesus preached from a boat (Matthew 13:2).
- Simon and Andrew and James and John left boats behind to follow Jesus (Mark 1:16–20).
- Jesus filled Peter's boat with so many fish the boat started to sink (John 21:4–8).

Can you think of others?

ourselves: *Is there something we've been slow to see about what Jesus is doing in our lives?*

Give Me a Sign! (8:11–13)

Next, the Pharisees came to question Jesus. They asked for "a sign from heaven" (8:11) as a test. Mark tells us, ". . . He sighed deeply in his spirit. . . " (8:12). They were seeking a spiritual verification, some kind of authentication of Jesus' divine connection.

Just as Jesus could not perform many miracles in his hometown because of the people's lack of belief (6:5–6), Jesus could not give a sign to the unbelieving Pharisees. On the one hand, this invites us to ponder the relationship of miracles and faith, but on the other hand this encounter points out that the Pharisees and the disciples were equally dense and slow to *get it* concerning Jesus.

The villagers of Jesus' hometown, the disciples who walked closely with Jesus, and the Pharisees all had access to the same knowledge, experiences, and conversations about Jesus and his miraculous works. They were all linked by their inability to see the divine in their midst. It is confounding to those who read this story with the privilege of two millennia of hindsight that these people could miss all the clues seemingly right before their eyes. Yet modern Christians are equally implicated in the sin of missing the work of God in our midst.

Watch Out (8:14–21)

Once again Mark takes us out on the water in a boat. Jesus and the disciples were in the boat with only one loaf of bread. Jesus gave a warning about the leavening power of the Pharisees, building on leaven as a metaphor for things that decay. It was commonly thought in Jesus' day that leaven was to be associated with decay, and so it was no surprise to hear Jesus alluding to the ways in which the Pharisaic system led to the spiritual decay of the Jewish people on the whole.

But, again, these dense disciples missed the meaning. They thought Jesus was criticizing them for failing to provision the boat with bread for the trip. They were focused on the temporal and physical while Jesus was trying to draw their attention to the spiritual threats that lurked around them.

Jesus' tone sounds frustrated as he headed into his speech about their hardheartedness. He was frustrated that they had confused physical bread for spiritual food. He was frustrated that they were assuming the one loaf of bread they had wouldn't be enough. Surely Jesus was thinking, *How can you not remember the feeding of the 4,000 Gentiles or the feeding of the 5,000 Jews?*

Jesus' words to the disciples verify that he was indeed frustrated. His questions of the disciples there in the boat must have shamed them. Yet Mark presents no evidence that they had gained insight, even with the confrontational questioning from Jesus. It is as though their world view was so deeply enmeshed in their collective psyche that they could see no reality other than the harsh one of their own experiences.

SEEING GOD

The Gospel of Mark aims to show us how people right around Jesus missed seeing God at work. Here are some practical tips to see God at work in your life:

- Watch for God in the natural world. Consider the movement of the stars, the changes of seasons, the winds of refreshment, and the storms of danger.
- Listen for God's activity in the words and actions of your closest family members. Take time to observe them, their passions, and their interests.
- Look for God at work in your community. Who is serving the poor, helping the homeless, driving the church bus, or caring for young children?
- Put down your technology and fast from e-mail, smart phones, internet, television, movies, radio, and other media for twenty-four hours.

It is possible that Mark was sending the message that the disciples could not understand Jesus apart from his death on the cross and subsequent resurrection. We have the benefit of that historical understanding, but they lacked a clear picture of the end game for Jesus. Nevertheless, they failed to see and understand. That is the bottom line.

Actions and Implications

The encounters in this lesson's focal passages must be grouped together if we are to *get it* today. We might avoid being *slow to get it* if we disciples could see that we have a continued need for humility in regard to faith. Moreover, we might also stand a greater chance of perceiving and understanding Jesus if we were willing to confess our failure to do so. In a circular sort of fashion, this humility feeds our faith and strengthens our resolve to follow Jesus.

Sometimes we are like the disciples. We see God at work all around us but still miss ways God is breaking into our world in every moment. Sometimes we are like the Pharisees, asking for a sign when the signs are already right in front of us.

QUESTIONS

1. This lesson focuses on four scenes from Mark. In what way(s) is Jesus hidden in plain sight in each of these scenes?
   - Jesus walks on water
   - Jesus feeds the 4,000
   - Jesus has a sharp encounter with the Pharisees
   - Jesus warns the disciples about the dangers of the leavening of the Pharisees

2. When Jesus walked on the water toward the disciples, they were terrified because they thought Jesus was a ghost. They were challenged in their faith. In what ways have you been scared when challenged in your faith?

3. How were the Pharisees and the disciples alike? How were they different?

4. Jesus expected his disciples to do something for the hungry 4,000. In essence he said, *You feed them*. In what ways might Jesus be calling you to tap into spiritual power in order to meet someone else's needs?

5. Do we demand too much of God when we ask for "a sign from heaven" (8:11) ourselves?

6. The disciples really missed the boat about the bread in the boat. What situations in your own life call for a closer inspection and more careful discernment to see how God is at work?

FOCAL TEXT
Mark 12:28–34

BACKGROUND
Mark 11:27—12:34

MAIN IDEA
Jesus taught that to love
God and one's neighbor
fully is at the heart of
the kingdom of God.

QUESTION TO EXPLORE
What *does* matter most in life?

STUDY AIM
To measure my life by what
Jesus said matters most

QUICK READ
Loving God wholeheartedly
and loving neighbors as
oneself matters most in the
kingdom of God. Following
Jesus allows entry into this
kingdom and makes possible
doing what matters most.

LESSON TEN
The Law Expert: Asking About What Matters Most

When I served as a hospital chaplain in a chemical dependency unit, the patients on that unit became my greatest teachers about the importance and difficulty of choosing what matters most. As with all of us, they knew what they should do, but they lacked the power to do it. They treated their frustrations with their always reliable, always deceptive drug of choice.

Slowly, drugs and alcohol came to matter more than anything else. Recovery began only when they recognized their helplessness and asked for help. Recovery was marked by a change in behavior regarding what *really* mattered most, their relationship to God and to others. They discovered the dramatic difference between *talking the talk* and *walking the walk*. Today's lesson invites us to look closely at our lives and to decide whether we *walk the walk* in obeying the greatest commandments.

The background for today's focal passage begins in Mark 11:27. Jesus was back in Jerusalem after his triumphant entry and cleansing the temple. As the religious leaders attempted to discredit Jesus, they asked him a series of questions focused on his right to speak with authority about the things of God.[1]

MARK 12:28-34

28 One of the teachers of the law came and heard them debating. Noticing that Jesus had given them a good answer, he asked him, "Of all the commandments, which is the most important?"

29 "The most important one," answered Jesus, "is this: 'Hear, O Israel, the Lord our God, the Lord is one. 30 Love the Lord your God with all your heart and with all your soul and with all your mind and with all your strength.' 31 The second is this: 'Love your neighbor as yourself.' There is no commandment greater than these."

32 "Well said, teacher," the man replied. "You are right in saying that God is one and there is no other but him. 33 To love him with all your heart, with all your understanding and with all your strength, and to love your neighbor as yourself is more important than all burnt offerings and sacrifices."

> [34] When Jesus saw that he had answered wisely, he said to him, "You are not far from the kingdom of God." And from then on no one dared ask him any more questions.

Loving God Completely (12:28–30)

The questioner in Mark 12:28 was "one of the teachers of the law." He was likely a Pharisee, and he probably had appreciated Jesus giving the Sadducees a "good answer" in the preceding debate about the resurrection. He would have believed in the resurrection in contrast to the Sadducees. He asked Jesus, "Of all the commandments, which is the most important?" The legal experts tended to answer this question in two different ways. The first way discouraged deciding that one commandment was more important than another. This approach had gotten more complicated as the laws had increased from the original ten given to Moses to 613. The other approach to this question was to positively summarize the law.[2]

Jesus used the positive summary when he answered the question regarding the most important of all the commandments. His direct answer was in sharp contrast to his responses to the crafty questions that had been posed earlier. Every Jew would have been familiar with Jesus' response: "Hear, O Israel, the Lord our God, the Lord is one." Mark was likely writing his Gospel to help the Christians in the city of Rome. The Romans believed in many gods, and the emperor even claimed to be a god. The confession that God was one, known as the *Shema*, would have been greatly appreciated by the church at Rome as they struggled with the daily challenges of dealing with a culture that did not embrace their God or their values.

Jesus reinforced the accepted belief that the most important command was to love God with the whole self. We will do well to remember that he said, "Do not think that I have come to abolish the Law or the Prophets; I have come not to abolish them but to fulfill them" (Matthew 5:17). The command to love God completely was the highest and best of the faith received from the Old Testament. This certainly covered the first four of the Ten Commandments (see Exodus 20:3–12). The requirement to love

God included doing so with the complete self: heart, soul, mind, and strength. The "heart" was considered to be the center for thinking. The will and feelings emerged from the "soul." The "mind" had to do with understanding and intelligence and sometimes was used similarly to the heart. "Strength" emphasizes both physical strength and the power of a person's being as well as all of their possessions. The word "all" is repeated four times for emphasis.[3] This command allowed for no part-time commitments.

This commandment still reminds us that what matters most is to love God beyond everything else. God should come before possessions, family, country, appetites, or self. This first commandment gives us the key that unlocks all of life. Forgetting self and giving ourselves unreservedly to God is the first command and leads to freedom and joy.

Loving Our Neighbor as Ourselves (12:31)

Then, Jesus combined the first and second commandments. The second commandment Jesus named, to "love your neighbor as yourself," also had developed prior to Jesus as a summary of all the law governing human relationships. This commandment included the last six of the Ten Commandments with their instruction to care for parents and the prohibitions against murder, adultery, stealing, lying, and coveting (Exod. 20:12–17). Jesus said that "Love your neighbor as yourself" covered these commands as well as all other laws governing treatment of others.

Jesus' answer to the question about what matters most was clear. God's people were to love God with an undivided heart and to love their neighbors as themselves.

The teacher of the law agreed completely with Jesus' answer. This teacher had given Jesus an easy question that allowed Jesus to once again make the point he had made in Mark 7:1–23. There, he pointed out that the religious leaders had altered the demands of the law by establishing traditions that they could achieve according to their interpretation. They knew how to wash their hands correctly, but with those same hands they took money unjustly. They talked of obeying the command to care for

THE KINGDOM OF GOD

The kingdom of God is deeply rooted in the Old Testament. The idea grew from believing God ruled over only Israel to an understanding that God ruled eternally over the whole universe. This rule included the present as well as the promise of a better age to come.

The kingdom of God was a central theme in Jesus' ministry and teaching. In Mark's Gospel alone, sayings regarding the kingdom occur a number of times. Jesus began his public ministry with the announcement: "The time has come. The kingdom of God is near. Repent and believe the good news!" (Mark 1:15). Throughout the Gospels the kingdom is presented as the present, growing, and coming reign of God among and within those who would trust themselves to God.[4]

Entry into the kingdom involves not simple acknowledgement of its existence but obedience to the King. "Follow me" remains Jesus' requirement for entering the kingdom (see Mark 10:21).

their parents, but they reinterpreted this law and pretended to honor God with their resources while not performing their duty to care for their parents.

Another insight into this encounter with the teacher of the law comes from the similar passage in Luke 10:25–37. In Luke's account the "expert in the law" wishing "to justify" himself asked Jesus, "and who is my neighbor" (Luke 10:29). In response, Jesus told the story of the Good Samaritan and forever changed the definition of a neighbor from the Old Testament understanding of the neighbor as "one of your people" (Leviticus 19:18) to the neighbor being anyone in need of help.

This command greatly challenges our divided hearts. The enormity of our neighbors' needs can cause us to choose not to obey this command. We see catastrophes happen and feel dwarfed by people's needs. Sadly, too often we are numbed by the depth and extent of human need. Worse, we may become angry with those in need because of the discomfort we feel and start blaming the victims. Too often, we get tied in knots about what we can't do and fail to reach out to those we are perfectly capable of helping.

CASE STUDY

Late at night your phone rings, and it's the teenage girl living next door. She says, "Daddy is really angry, and we are scared. Can you help us?" How could you best be neighbor to this young girl and to her family? What should you do?

"Not Far From" but Not There Yet (12:32–34)

The teacher of the law was impressed with Jesus' response. He repeated Jesus' answer, adding only that the two commands were more important than "all burnt offerings and sacrifices." This man showed great insight and awareness of what mattered most. Yet, he had not gotten the whole picture. His response to Jesus was that of an equal and not that of a disciple. Nevertheless, Jesus was impressed with this man's acknowledgement of what was most important. Then, he said to him, "You are not far from the kingdom of God." Mark ended this section abruptly with the comment, "from then on no one dared ask him any more questions."

The larger context of this account helps to understand this verse. Although this questioner was presented in a very positive light, his question was one in a series in which the Pharisees and Sadducees were trying to trap Jesus into saying something contrary to either Roman or Jewish law. Perhaps this teacher, too, was trying to trap Jesus, although Mark gave no indication of that. Nevertheless, he likely was left with a lot to ponder when Jesus gave him both a blessing and a confrontation: "You are not far from the kingdom of God." This man with his high view of the biblical law and his standing as a teacher of that law probably thought he was already in the kingdom and one of its chief representatives. Jesus, on the other hand, while blessing him said, in effect, *You are well on your way to what matters most, but you aren't there yet.*

Before we judge this man too quickly, we must remember that the disciples themselves had not yet grasped what lay ahead for Jesus. This conversation with the expert in the law happened during the last week before the crucifixion. The disciples still were entertaining ideas of an earthly kingdom of God. Yet, the reality was that the most decisive event in the kingdom of God was just about to happen. The one who had come to save his people was about to be put to death by them.

This teacher of the law could not have been an expert in what was about to happen and could not have conceived of what would be required to be in the kingdom rather than "not far" from it. On the other hand, we can better understand this because we know what happened next. We understand that fully loving God and fully loving our neighbor involves following Jesus and obeying him. The expert in the law was able to acknowledge what mattered most, but he had not yet heard or responded to Jesus' command to follow him. Acknowledgement of truth is a wonderful first step. Obedience to truth is essential to being a part of the kingdom of God.

Implications and Actions

We need to recognize that we too may be "not far from the kingdom of God," but we can also recognize that entry into the kingdom of God comes as we follow Jesus and accept his grace, forgiveness, and power. As with the people to whom Mark wrote in first-century Rome, we are continually asked to adopt the values of the society around us. We are tempted to treat this world as mattering most rather than to let ourselves be transformed into people who demonstrate what loving God with our whole being means and how caring for our neighbors can make a better world. We know what matters most. However, we receive power to do what matters most only when we allow Jesus to rule within our lives. Entry into the kingdom of God allows us to *walk the walk* and not just *talk the talk*.

QUESTIONS

1. What keeps us from giving God first place in our lives?

2. How do we balance self-care and caring for others?

3. How do you determine who your neighbor is?

4. Why is the belief in the kingdom of God important for daily living?

5. What are some specific ways you can better love God with "all" of yourself?

NOTES

1. Unless otherwise indicated, all Scripture quotations in lessons 1–6, 10–11 are taken from the HOLY BIBLE, NEW INTERNATIONAL VERSION®. Copyright © 1973, 1978, 1984 Biblica.

2. See William L. Lane, "The Gospel According to Mark," *The New International Commentary on the New Testament* (Grand Rapids, Michigan: William B. Eerdmans Publishing Company, 1974), 431–432.

3. See David E. Garland, "Mark," *The NIV Application Commentary* (Grand Rapids, Michigan: Zondervan Publishing House, 1996), 483–485.

4. O.E. Evans, "Kingdom of God, of Heaven," *The Interpreter's Dictionary of the Bible*, vol. 3 (Nashville, Tennessee: Abingdon Press, 1962), 17–25.

FOCAL TEXT
Mark 14:1–9

BACKGROUND
Mark 14:1–9

MAIN IDEA

As Jesus approached the crucifixion, a woman anointed him with expensive ointment, an act that Jesus praised as being in honor of his burial.

QUESTION TO EXPLORE

How much is too much in showing honor to Jesus?

STUDY AIM

To measure how I serve Jesus by how the woman at Bethany served him

QUICK READ

Jesus gratefully received the extravagant anointing by the woman at Bethany and defended her action against those focused on more obvious needs. He utilized her gift to prepare for his death and burial.

LESSON ELEVEN
The Woman at Bethany: Honoring Jesus Extravagantly

Ernest Evans gave me a life-changing gift. He was a small farmer, cabinetmaker, and devout Nazarene Christian who lived near our dairy farm in Arkansas. He asked me to come to see him when I was about seventeen years old and had just entered the ministry. When I arrived at his house, he brought out a box of books, a sixteen-volume set of Alexander MacLaren's *Expositions of Holy Scripture*. He said, "I love these books, but you will use them more than I." I thanked him, but I had no idea of what he had given me. I glanced at the books and put them in my closet.

About three years later, I began serving my first small church as pastor. The congregation informed me it was time for the summer revival meeting, and the pastor always did the preaching. I had preached all six of my sermons. Desperate, I remembered the books in my closet. Alexander MacLaren lived again! Moreover, I was imprinted with the respect for the Bible and skill of a man that I later learned was one of the most gifted preachers in Christian history. Ernest Evans changed my life by giving me something precious to him.

Today's Scripture reveals the importance of an extravagant gift during the tension-filled week before the crucifixion. Jesus blessed the woman at Bethany who honored him with an extravagant gift. Remembering this woman's gift will help us to better measure our own giving and assist us in expressing our love for God.

MARK 14:1–9

¹ Now the Passover and the Feast of Unleavened Bread were only two days away, and the chief priests and the teachers of the law were looking for some sly way to arrest Jesus and kill him. ² "But not during the Feast," they said, "or the people may riot."

³ While he was in Bethany, reclining at the table in the home of a man known as Simon the Leper, a woman came with an alabaster jar of very expensive perfume, made of pure nard. She broke the jar and poured the perfume on his head.

⁴ Some of those present were saying indignantly to one another, "Why this waste of perfume? ⁵ It could have been sold for more than a year's wages and the money given to the poor." And they rebuked her harshly.

> [6] "Leave her alone," said Jesus. "Why are you bothering her? She has done a beautiful thing to me. [7] The poor you will always have with you, and you can help them any time you want. But you will not always have me. [8] She did what she could. She poured perfume on my body beforehand to prepare for my burial. [9] I tell you the truth, wherever the gospel is preached throughout the world, what she has done will also be told, in memory of her."

Loving Without Reservation (14:1–3)

"The Passover and the Feast of Unleavened Bread were only two days away," and Jesus' enemies were looking for a "sly" way to arrest him and to kill him. They were afraid to arrest Jesus during Passover because of the large crowds present and because of Jesus' popularity. They stood a good chance of the whole plot backfiring and being blamed by the Roman government for a riot.

Meanwhile, Jesus and his disciples were at Bethany. This small village lay just over a mile and a half east of Jerusalem on the eastern slope of the Mount of Olives. Mary, Martha, and Lazarus lived there, and the woman of Bethany in our lesson today might have been Mary (see John 12:1–8).

Jesus had to be feeling great stress. He understood that the praise he had received on entering Jerusalem a few days earlier would not last. He was fully aware of the hatred of the chief priests and teachers of the law. He knew he was going to die soon. Jesus was human as well as divine and had the same dread of pain, suffering, and death that we all have. He also was alone. None of the disciples could yet conceive of the total disruption and loss of their dreams that lay immediately ahead.

One person did appreciate something of what Jesus was facing. The woman at Bethany appeared to have appreciated the fact that he needed ministry and care. She also might have consciously chosen to honor Jesus as the Messiah, the Anointed One, and to take matters into her own hands. More likely, she was wholeheartedly devoted to Jesus and treated him as an honored guest who needed support, reverence, and respect.

The woman's actions stand in sharp contrast to the treachery of the chief priest and the teachers of the law and the agreement of Judas to betray Jesus. Their plotting brackets the only recorded act of kindness and gratitude given to him during this week before his death. The self-forgetful anointing provided by this woman shines brightly against the dark background of their actions. She gave him an exceedingly precious and expensive gift. Likely the nard, an aromatic oil extracted from a root native to India, was a family heirloom passed from one generation to another. The value of the perfume was about equal to a year's wages for a laborer.

This woman stands out as an example of devotion and sensitivity. The rest of the disciples seemed to be doing business as usual. They could have easily been celebrating the popular acclaim Jesus had received and were still hopeful of positions for themselves. The woman, however, was overwhelmed with gratitude and concern for Jesus, whom she loved without reservation. Her love for Jesus took away her self-interest, and she gave extravagantly. Her love and gratitude for Jesus was unlimited, and her gift was without calculation of cost. Her example can lead us to open our hearts without reservation.

The Practicality of Impracticality (14:4–7)

As the fragrance of the nard filled the room, the disciples erupted with angry criticism. They complained that the perfume could have at least been sold and the proceeds given to the poor. The woman's gift appeared to be terribly impractical. "Why this waste of perfume?" seemed like a reasonable question. Their perspective was limited on this occasion, but there was foundation to their objections based in tradition and biblical command. Giving to the poor was expected of the people of Israel (see Deut. 15:1–11). Likely this was on their minds since giving to the poor was an important part of observing the Passover.[1]

Jesus quickly defended the woman. He said, "She has done a beautiful thing to me." The Greek word translated "beautiful" can also mean *useful.* Here, it had both meanings. Then, Jesus said, "The poor you will always have with you," based on Deuteronomy 15:11. These words have been misused to justify not caring for the poor. Quite to the contrary, Jesus expressed great compassion for the poor in his ministry. He was

THE PASSOVER IN JERUSALEM

The Passover commemorated God's deliverance of Israel from Egypt when the Israelites were spared the plague that killed the first born of the Egyptians. During the first century, the Jews continued the practice of using the blood of a lamb and observing the ritual Passover feast to recall that Passover night in Egypt. At the Passover season, which included the seven-day Feast of the Unleavened Bread, huge crowds swelled Jerusalem's population. Between 85,000 and 300,000 pilgrims flooded this city of 60,000 to 120,000 people. Religious and nationalistic fervor heated to a fever pitch. Well aware of the potential of rebellion at the time of the Passover, the Roman governor would transfer additional soldiers and his headquarters from Caesarea on the Mediterranean coast to Jerusalem. Both the Roman and Jewish leaders worked to avoid any unusual disruptions during Passover. In spite of their efforts, the most significant disruption in history occurred with the crucifixion of Jesus as he became the Passover sacrifice for all people.[2]

clear that provision of food for the hungry, drink for the thirsty, clothes for the needy, and comfort for those sick or imprisoned was a direct gift to him. He said, "I tell you the truth, whatever you did for one of the least of these brothers of mine, you did for me" (Matthew 25:40).

Giving to the poor remains a priority. Since Jesus is not physically present, our opportunity to love extravagantly is now to give to the poor. The poor may be those who are without money, jobs, education, or health care, as well as those who live in the poverty of not having a personal relationship with Jesus. Are we tempted to say with the disciples, "Why this waste?" when we think of giving to the least of these?

Jesus then went further in providing justification for what seemed an impractical gift. It appears that this woman alone recognized his poverty and in anointing him she was giving to the poor. She may have understood more than any of the men the desperate situation that was converging on him. She could not have understood everything, but Jesus received her gift and deepened its meaning by saying this anointing was in preparation for his burial.

The extravagant gift of the woman at Bethany became a gift of great importance and practicality as Jesus approached the cross. He died the death of a criminal. Criminals were not permitted to be anointed after death.

The Jewish law held that the highest duty was to attend to the dead since the window of opportunity was narrow and other duties such as giving to the poor could be delayed until later opportunity. While the opportunity existed, this woman anointed one who was as good as dead. Her example reminds us to do what we can when we can even if it doesn't measure up to other people's standards of practicality.

Doing What You Can (14:8–9)

Jesus also said of the woman and her gift, "She did what she could." If the woman was Mary, the sister of Lazarus, we have learned elsewhere that she seemed less practical than her sister, Martha (see Luke 10:38–42). In the story in John 12:1–8, Martha was serving dinner and Mary poured the perfume on Jesus. Martha once again was doing something practical. Meanwhile, Mary did something that was her own deep expression of love, and Jesus blessed her for it.

Jesus affirmed not only the gift that the woman at Bethany gave but also her giftedness. Some can serve tables like Martha, some can build tables, and others can provide the food that the table holds. Jesus asks us to be ourselves and give the gifts we have rather than trying to become someone other than who we are.

Jesus also affirmed that she did what was possible in the moment. She could not do everything, but she could do something. Jesus received what she did as a gift of love. As he received it, he transformed it into more than she could have imagined. Jesus said, "She did what she could." Doing what she could, she performed one of the highest duties imaginable in the Jewish culture. She anointed Jesus for his burial.

None of us can do everything, but all of us can do something. Doing what you can may not seem extravagant to you, but in God's hands it can be transformed into more than you can imagine. God can change even small acts of kindness to those who suffer into life-changing gifts. Doing what we can to honor Jesus will always be honored by him.

CASE STUDY

You have become acquainted with a woman who cleans homes for a living. You learn that both she and her husband lost good jobs during the recession. Her husband, a public school teacher, subsequently became disabled. They lost their home and now cannot pay the rent on their present home. They are moving to substandard housing in a crime-ridden area. They are in real danger of being crushed by their poverty. Does giving extravagantly to Jesus have anything to do with your response to this woman and her needs?

Implications for life

Outside observers would probably wonder at the gifts of love that are shared in my Bible study class. Teachers give hours of time in preparing, teaching, and leading. Others make sure that communication occurs with e-mail and the church website. Others consistently see that food is prepared and served. Others lead in missions and ministry to the sick and poor.

Are such acts extravagant? Maybe it doesn't seem so, but all of this represents time and resources that make a profound difference in the quality of life of those who are touched by this fellowship. The extravagant gift of the woman at Bethany blessed Jesus and became an enduring memorial and encouragement.

Ernest Evans's gift to me changed my life and ministry. We can trust that God can take every gift that honors him and make more of it than we can ever imagine.

QUESTIONS

1. How does the example of the woman at Bethany encourage you to give extravagantly?

2. What are some ways Christians can be hospitable to those in need?

3. Since we will always have the poor among us, what should we do?

4. How does careful calculation sometimes get in the way of responding in love to others?

NOTES

1. See William L. Lane, *The Gospel According to Mark*, The New International Commentary on the New Testament (Grand Rapids, Michigan: William B. Eerdmans Publishing Company, 1974), 493–495.

2. David E. Garland, *Mark*, The NIV Application Commentary (Grand Rapids, Michigan: Zondervan Publishing House, 1996), 513–514.

FOCAL TEXT
Mark 14:10–11, 17–21, 41–50

BACKGROUND
Mark 3:14–19a; 14:1–2,
10–11, 17–21, 32–50

MAIN IDEA
Judas committed the
unthinkable act of betraying
Jesus, who had chosen him
and with whom he had
journeyed for many months.

QUESTION TO EXPLORE
Is it I?

STUDY AIM
To contrast Judas's actions
to the actions of Jesus and
to ask myself, "Is it I?"

QUICK READ
After journeying with Jesus
and hearing him teach many
times about the kingdom
of God, Judas, one of Jesus'
closest followers, betrayed him.

Imagine being there when Jesus fed the 5,000. Imagine looking out across the Sea of Galilee and being terrified because of witnessing Jesus walk on the water in the midst of the storm. Imagine being one of the first to sit among the crowds in first-century Galilee and hear some of the most profound teachings ever uttered by a human being. Imagine that you are one of the ones who got to see first hand the joy and salvation that Jesus brought to some of the most despised people in society. Now imagine that you are the person to bring all of this to a halt. You are the disciple, the fellow companion of Jesus of Nazareth, who betrays him and delivers him into the hands of his enemies.

What was Judas thinking that would have put him on such a different trajectory than his Rabbi and Savior, Jesus? Perhaps the more important issues to explore have to do with our own relationship to Jesus and what Jesus desires to accomplish among us in our own time.

Is it I who think that my way is better? Is it I who allow selfish motives to cloud God's will for my life and the lives of those around me? Is it I who get in the way of God's purpose for my church? Is it I?[1]

MARK 14:10–11, 17–21, 41–50

[10] Then Judas Iscariot, who was one of the twelve, went to the chief priests in order to betray him to them. [11] When they heard it, they were greatly pleased, and promised to give him money. So he began to look for an opportunity to betray him.

• •

[17] When it was evening, he came with the twelve. [18] And when they had taken their places and were eating, Jesus said, "Truly I tell you, one of you will betray me, one who is eating with me." [19] They began to be distressed and to say to him one after another, "Surely, not I?" [20] He said to them, "It is one of the twelve, one who is dipping bread into the bowl with me. [21] For the Son of Man goes as it is written of him, but woe to that one by whom the Son of Man is betrayed! It would have been better for that one not to have been born."

• •

> ⁴¹ He came a third time and said to them, "Are you still sleeping and taking your rest? Enough! The hour has come; the Son of Man is betrayed into the hands of sinners. ⁴² Get up, let us be going. See, my betrayer is at hand."
>
> ⁴³ Immediately, while he was still speaking, Judas, one of the twelve, arrived; and with him there was a crowd with swords and clubs, from the chief priests, the scribes, and the elders. ⁴⁴ Now the betrayer had given them a sign, saying, "The one I will kiss is the man; arrest him and lead him away under guard." ⁴⁵ So when he came, he went up to him at once and said, "Rabbi!" and kissed him. ⁴⁶ Then they laid hands on him and arrested him. ⁴⁷ But one of those who stood near drew his sword and struck the slave of the high priest, cutting off his ear. ⁴⁸ Then Jesus said to them, "Have you come out with swords and clubs to arrest me as though I were a bandit? ⁴⁹ Day after day I was with you in the temple teaching, and you did not arrest me. But let the scriptures be fulfilled." ⁵⁰ All of them deserted him and fled.

Betrayal from Within (14:10–11)

Mark's Gospel gives the reader no motive for why Judas betrayed Jesus. The only thing mentioned in Mark's account is that the chief priests promised to give Judas money for his cooperation in their scheme. Another hint at Judas's motive might very well be connected with what happened just prior to Judas deciding to betray Jesus. We're told that some of the disciples became angry and scolded the woman for her apparent waste of the costly ointment (see lesson 11 on Mark 14:4–5; see also Matthew 26:8–9). The main point of contention was over the value of the ointment and how money from selling it could have presumably gone toward a more practical cause such as caring for the poor. Although Judas's act of betrayal does not come immediately after a similar story in John 12:1–8, the Gospel of John specifically names Judas as the one who got angry about the wasted ointment. We then get a quick aside about Judas that is not found in either Matthew or Mark. John tells us that Judas really didn't care about the poor at all, but that he was a thief and regularly stole from the disciples' common purse of which he was in charge.

All of these things taken together, including Judas receiving money for his betrayal, give us a picture of a greedy thief. Could Judas's motive for betraying his master have really been one of mere greed?

It is likely that Judas's attention was still so focused on the transitory that he was unable to see the true and everlasting riches that would come with the establishment of God's kingdom. Jesus was teaching about something new and radical, something that would turn the world on its head. Judas was still thinking about the status quo. Perhaps he was looking forward to the riches that were sure to come with establishing an earthly kingdom and when it was clear that this wasn't going to happen, he became completely disillusioned. If this is the case, then Judas's actions serve as an example of Paul's stern warning in 1 Timothy 6:9–10: "But those who want to be rich fall into temptation and are trapped by many senseless and harmful desires that plunge people into ruin and destruction. For the love of money is a root of all kinds of evil, and in their eagerness to be rich some have wandered away from the faith and pierced themselves with many pains."

So often God's vision and what God really cares about are far removed from our narrow-minded ideas and concerns. Jesus was thinking about the big picture, while Judas could see only in human terms. Let us remember that if Judas could be lured away from his Savior and Lord by his pet sin, then so can we.

Not a Victim, but a Prophet (14:17–21)

Whatever Judas's motive might have been for betraying Jesus, we know that Jesus was not caught off guard. He knew and accepted that he would be betrayed, handed over to the authorities, and crucified by the Romans. What must surely have been disappointing and difficult to take was that he would be handed over by a close companion, "one of the twelve" (Mark 14:20). There they sat in one of the most intimate contexts of ancient Jewish culture: around a common meal; together, praying, touching the same food, meeting one another's eyes, sharing a closeness and trust that few did with Jesus. They had been through quite a lot together, and most if not all of them thought that a glorious ending was near. The

---

JUDAS ISCARIOT: AN OVERVIEW

Judas is such an obscure personality in the Gospels that even the proper meaning of his name is difficult to determine. Out of the several possibilities for the meaning of *Iscariot*, scholars think the most likely meaning is, *man of Kerioth*. If this is in fact the meaning then this means that Judas was the only Judean among the twelve disciples.

The exact reason for Judas's betrayal of Jesus is impossible to determine with any certainty. In addition to greed (see comments on Mark 14:10–11), Bible scholars have suggested two other possibilities. One is that Judas had grown disillusioned with Jesus as a Messianic figure and wanted to abandon ship before Jesus allowed himself and his movement to be destroyed. Another thought is that Judas had not lost faith in Jesus at all, but that he was trying to force Jesus to act by putting him in danger.

It is worth noting that the Gospels tell us that Judas "repented" (Matt. 27:3; "felt remorse," NASB) and tried to give back the money he'd accepted for betraying Jesus. Judas later hung himself (Matt. 27:5) and was buried in what came to be known as the "Field of Blood" (Matt. 27:8).

Romans would be utterly defeated; Jesus would establish the most powerful kingdom in history; and the Jews would rule the world. Judas wanted something different from Jesus' purpose, and Jesus knew it.

Jesus' words in this passage may have been meant to stir Judas, to bring him back. Notice that it says that the "Son of Man goes as it is written of him" (14:21), but it is not written that *Judas* must betray Jesus. Nothing was forcing Judas to sin, but only his own hard-heartedness. Jesus must be handed over, but woe to the one who took such action. "It would be better for that one not to have been born," Jesus said. Judas was responsible for his actions. There is no escaping responsibility for the choices we make and the consequences that come with those choices.

As Jesus Said It Would Be: Betrayal and Desertion (14:41–50)

Next, Mark made a swift transition into his account of the Lord's Supper (14:22–25). Then after singing a hymn (all of or parts of Psalms

115—118), Jesus and his disciples headed to the Mount of Olives (Mark 14:26). There Jesus gave them all some bad news (14:27–30). Quoting Zechariah 13:7, he told them that they would all desert him, but that after he was raised up he would go on before them to Galilee. All of the disciples protested this, especially Peter. Jesus countered the protests by informing Peter that Peter would in fact deny him three different times before the cock crowed twice.

Although the disciples appeared to be courageous enough to go to prison or die with their Messiah, they were not disciplined enough to stay awake and pray with him. The content of Jesus' prayer in the Garden of Gethsemane is instructive for the church. Jesus affirmed that for God all things are possible and asked to be spared the suffering and humiliation of the cross. It is, however, God's will and not ours that matters most. So it is God's will that must be done.

On three different occasions Jesus found Peter, James, and John sleeping. When they were awakened the third and last time, danger had entered the garden. The "betrayer" was at hand.

As is typical of the Gospel of Mark, the word "immediately" in 14:43 relentlessly moves the story forward, telling us that while Jesus was still speaking Judas arrived with an armed crowd. Still thinking that Jesus was unaware of his scheme, Judas approached him with the greeting of a kiss, which was so typical, especially between a rabbi and his pupil. Thus, ironically with the sign of intimacy and respect, Judas unleashed his evil intentions for his close companion of more than three years. As planned, the kiss resulted in Jesus' arrest, but the fact that this *must* happen was still unclear to his disciples.

LESSONS FROM JUDAS

- Pray for God to help you identify any false expectations you may have of Jesus.
- Search your heart for any trace of greed. Explore how God wants you to deal with this desire.
- Identify those parts of Jesus' teaching that you are most often tempted to abandon.
- Ask Jesus to forgive you for abandoning him

At least one disciple felt that if there was ever an appropriate time to begin fighting for their teacher and their cause, it was now. The Gospel of Mark gives the most abbreviated account of this story. We're merely told, "One of those who stood near drew his sword and struck the slave of the high priest, cutting off his ear" (Mark 14:47).

Jesus expressed dismay over his enemies' paranoid approach to arresting him. Why arrest him in the middle of the night armed with swords and clubs when he was with them in the temple day after day? Jesus' final words in this passage confirm that his heart was aligned with the words on his lips, for he had prayed in the garden just minutes before: "Yet, not what I want, but what you want" (14:36). Jesus said, ". . . Let the Scriptures be fulfilled" (14:49).

While Jesus' disciples might have been willing to fight for Jesus, they were certainly not willing to stand idly by, get arrested, and die with him without a fight. That Judas betrayed Jesus is a cold, hard fact. In addition to that betrayal every one of Jesus' disciples deserted him in the end.

While at first glance verses 51–52 may seem like a random, if not bizarre, detail, the verse actually serves to highlight just how abandoned Jesus was. This "young man" whoever he was, would rather give up his clothing and suffer the shame of being found naked than to be identified with Jesus. These verses may also serve as a symbol of the shame of all of the disciples who abandoned their Lord. They did indeed "all become deserters" (14:27).

Implications and Actions

Did Judas betray Jesus out of pure greed? Likely a number of factors shaped Judas's motive or motives. While we will never fully know what Judas was thinking or why he did what he did, we do have access to the voices in our own heads. What thoughts and plans draw us away from Christ's purposes for our lives? Some of them may very well make sense. Some of our plans may fit right in with our goals and values. But do our goals and values match those of our Lord? This is the question that we must be vigilant in asking.

QUESTIONS

1. In your view, what compelled Judas to betray Jesus?

2. What are some ways that the modern church is tempted to betray Jesus?

3. Can any defense be made for the disciples' abandonment of Jesus?

4. Is the story of Judas's betrayal of Jesus applicable for Christians today? Why or why not? How?

NOTES

1. Unless otherwise indicated, all Scripture quotations on the back cover, in "Introducing The Gospel of Mark: People Responding to Jesus," in lessons 7—9, 12–13, and in the Christmas lesson are taken from the New Revised Standard Version Bible.

FOCAL TEXT
Mark 15:40—16:8

BACKGROUND
Mark 15:25—16:8

MAIN IDEA
Women were faithfully present at Jesus' crucifixion, his burial, and the empty tomb.

QUESTION TO EXPLORE
Would you have been there?

STUDY AIM
To state the significance of the presence of the women at Jesus' crucifixion, his burial, and the empty tomb

QUICK READ
Some of Jesus' most faithful followers were women. A few of these women served as eyewitnesses to his crucifixion, burial, and resurrection.

LESSON THIRTEEN
Women at the Cross and the Tomb: Serving Jesus to the End

Growing up I had great admiration for He-Man. Yes, the cartoon character. I admired the guy because he was so much like me. Together we flexed our muscles and were quite capable of defeating the forces of evil with brute strength. He wasn't the only man I admired. Along with He-Man there were some *real* guys too. Guys like Rocky, MacGyver, Indiana Jones, Rambo, and Superman. Together we beat up the bad guys, we saved the day, we were the heroes people could count on.

As I grew up I began to notice that men didn't have the corner on strength. I also, came to understand that there were different kinds of strength. So while I still enjoy watching my favorite heroes bring justice to villains, I have also benefited greatly from the kind of strength that comes from a woman trying to keep her family together. I've learned about a quiet strength that is coupled with stubborn persistence in a woman who worked her way through college as a single mother. I have witnessed a woman forgive seventy times seven. My mother is a trooper. I can only hope to demonstrate half the strength she has in my own lifetime.

I continue to learn about strength and faithfulness from the women in my life—my mother, my wife, my daughter. I thank God every day that God did not leave us men to our own devices. Women have and will continue to influence the course of history in profound ways. This reality was also true in the life and ministry of Jesus Christ.

MARK 15:40–47

40 There were also women looking on from a distance; among them were Mary Magdalene, and Mary the mother of James the younger and of Joses, and Salome. 41 These used to follow him and provided for him when he was in Galilee; and there were many other women who had come up with him to Jerusalem.

42 When evening had come, and since it was the day of Preparation, that is, the day before the sabbath, 43 Joseph of Arimathea, a respected member of the council, who was also himself waiting expectantly for the kingdom of God, went boldly to Pilate and asked for the body of Jesus. 44 Then Pilate wondered

if he were already dead; and summoning the centurion, he asked him whether he had been dead for some time. [45] When he learned from the centurion that he was dead, he granted the body to Joseph. [46] Then Joseph bought a linen cloth, and taking down the body, wrapped it in the linen cloth, and laid it in a tomb that had been hewn out of the rock. He then rolled a stone against the door of the tomb. [47] Mary Magdalene and Mary the mother of Joses saw where the body was laid.

MARK 16:1–8

[1] When the sabbath was over, Mary Magdalene, and Mary the mother of James, and Salome bought spices, so that they might go and anoint him. [2] And very early on the first day of the week, when the sun had risen, they went to the tomb. [3] They had been saying to one another, "Who will roll away the stone for us from the entrance to the tomb?" [4] When they looked up, they saw that the stone, which was very large, had already been rolled back. [5] As they entered the tomb, they saw a young man, dressed in a white robe, sitting on the right side; and they were alarmed. [6] But he said to them, "Do not be alarmed; you are looking for Jesus of Nazareth, who was crucified. He has been raised; he is not here. Look, there is the place they laid him. [7] But go, tell his disciples and Peter that he is going ahead of you to Galilee; there you will see him, just as he told you." [8] So they went out and fled from the tomb, for terror and amazement had seized them; and they said nothing to anyone, for they were afraid.

Looking On: Jesus of Nazareth Who Was Crucified (15:40–47)

"It was nine o'clock in the morning when they crucified him" (Mark 15:25). The charge against him was that he was "The King of the Jews" (15:26). Jesus' morning was spent between two bandits who were crucified on either side of him. As for his opponents, it was not enough for them to witness his gruesome death penalty carried out. While hanging on the cross, Jesus was mocked and taunted by the common people, the chief priests, and even the two criminals who were crucified with him. The spiritual darkness over all of these events was matched by a physical darkness that came over the whole land at noon and lasted until three o'clock (15:33). It was at this time that Jesus, feeling completely forsaken, gave a loud cry and took his last breath. Although there must have been several who were present when Jesus died, Mark emphasizes a lone centurion who, ironically, recognized Jesus as "the Son of God" (15:39).

Where was everyone else? Where were Peter and the rest of the disciples who just hours before were so passionately saying they would die with their Lord if they had to? According to Mark's Gospel they were nowhere to be found.

We do not find complete abandonment on the part of Jesus' followers, however. A group of women were looking on at these tragic events from a distance. Although these women do not receive much attention in the Gospels, we know that they played a crucial role in Jesus' ministry, providing him with financial support (Mark 15:41; Luke 8:2–3). This should remind us of the importance of individuals extending help to others. Moreover, many who get only a footnote or no mention at all have made sacrificial contributions to our lives, directly or indirectly.

WOMEN IN WORSHIP

Jewish worship practices serve as indicators of how women were thought of before and during the time of Jesus. For example, Jewish women could not go much farther into the temple than Gentiles could. A specific court for women was designated in the temple, and they could go no farther into the temple. Areas beyond this court were off limits to them.

There were certain restrictions for women in synagogue worship as well. In fact, just to get a synagogue built in a community required ten males who were at least thirteen years of age. If the town had eight males who were of age and fifty women, no synagogue! Women were also separated from the men during synagogue worship and were prevented from having any kind of official authoritative role in the religious life of the community.

Although their names are forgotten, their influences cannot be hidden or so easily dismissed.

These seemingly peripheral women were not so peripheral here at the end. They stood at a distance as their Savior died, and their faith did not falter. As heart-wrenching as it was, the women looked on and did not abandon their Lord.

After Jesus took his last breath, the ordeal was not over. A number of matters still had to be handled. Although the spectacle of the crucifixion was over, it seems the women could not tear themselves away from the scene. They remained near throughout the task of Jesus' burial. Mark tells us that Joseph of Arimathea played a key role in making sure that Jesus' body was properly buried, putting himself at great risk to do so. He asked Pilate for Jesus' body. He bought a linen cloth and wrapped Jesus' body in it. He laid Jesus' body in a tomb and then rolled a stone over the door of the tomb.

As before, the disciples that we read so much about earlier in the Gospel were nowhere to be found. Mary Magdalene, Mary the mother of James the younger and Joses, and Salome, however, remained until Joseph gave the very last push on the rock that rolled into place to cover the door of the tomb.

Looking Up: He Has Been Raised (16:1–8)

Mary Magdalene, Mary the mother of James, and Salome were still not finished. They returned to the tomb after the Sabbath was over in order to demonstrate their faithfulness in the final act of anointing Jesus' body with spices. They soon found that their question about who would roll the stone away from the entrance of the tomb was irrelevant. They got quite an unexpected surprise when they saw that it had already been done. Also irrelevant were their plans for a corpse. The only person inside the tomb was alive and well. The "young man" who was dressed in a white robe and "sitting on the right side" gave the women quite a scare and informed them there was no reason to fear.

So these women who had come into the tomb to honor the dead received the new task of going out and proclaiming that the power of death had been overturned through the resurrection of Jesus Christ. This Jesus who was crucified has been raised! Specifically, the women

> ## GALATIANS 3:28–29
>
> One morning during Sunday School someone reads Galatians 3:28–29 and asks you what it means for there to no longer be male or female. What do you tell them? Does your answer relate at all to today's lesson? Why or why not?

were instructed to tell Peter and the rest of the disciples that they would find Jesus in Galilee. This should ring familiar since Jesus told them that after he was raised up he would go before them into Galilee (Mark 14:28). This fact is confirmed by the Gospel of John when Jesus showed himself to the disciples by the Sea of Tiberias (John 21).

It is certainly worth noting the significance of women being the first of anyone in the world to go and tell about the resurrection of Jesus Christ. Although it is difficult for us to imagine in twenty-first century America, most of the time in ancient Jewish culture the testimony of a woman or any group of women for that matter counted for absolutely nothing. Therefore, in addition to the women at the empty tomb reporting the unbelievable, their testimony was also questionable because of the very fact that they were women. The Gospel of Luke gives us a glimpse into this notion (Luke 24:8–11).

Another point regarding the testimony of the women concerning the resurrection of Jesus is that this thought could have very well been embarrassing for some in the early church. After all, the first people to serve as witnesses to the single most important event in history were women, women whose eyewitness testimony didn't really count for anything. That surely would have made the accounts of the resurrection in the Gospels seem dubious to some readers. However, modern scholars have indicated that since women are reported as being the first eyewitnesses, this actually lends more credibility to the story. That is to say that if the early church *had* made up the resurrection story, they certainly would not have recorded that women were the first witnesses, but men.

Throughout this study of Mark's Gospel we have encountered a number of responses to Jesus. There were those who played an important role in preparation such as John the Baptist. There were also those who tragically misunderstood the significance of Jesus. This is evident in the kinds of responses that come from Peter, James and John, the people of Jesus' hometown, the disciples, the religious leaders, and Judas Iscariot. And then there were those who could testify of the power of Jesus to change their lives: Levi, the disturbed man in the tombs, Jairus and the woman who had suffered for twelve years, the expert in the law, and the woman at Bethany. In addition to all of these we must not forget the women who were faithfully present at Jesus' crucifixion, burial, and resurrection, for it was through them that the gospel first began to be spread. That first testimony of Jesus' resurrection is still being given to this day. Jesus' resurrection power lives on.

Implications and Actions

It's no secret that faith today is still filled with ups and downs. How would you characterize your faith? Are you like Peter, who was quick to think that he knew what was best only to find that his understanding and commitment were rather shallow? Or does your faith reflect the unassuming and steady faithfulness of these women? My hunch is that most of us are somewhere in between. The story of these women's faithfulness serves to remind us that our faith in Christ is always rewarded with surprise, joy, and hope no matter how dark things seem to us. We should stay the course because God can make a way.

QUESTIONS

1. How have the roles of women changed since the times of Jesus? Do you think women receive enough credit for the strength and faithfulness they demonstrate in difficult times?

2. What do you think accounts for the steadfast faith of these women?

3. Mark 16:8 says that the women "fled from the tomb, for terror and amazement had seized them." Why do you think the women were so afraid?

4. As you think back over the course of this study, with which character in Mark's Gospel do you most identify? Review the contents page to refresh your memory about all of the people studied.

FOCAL TEXT
Matthew 1:18–25

BACKGROUND
Matthew 1:18–25

MAIN IDEA
Jesus the Christ, who is God with us, came to bring salvation.

QUESTION TO EXPLORE
What does Jesus' birth mean?

STUDY AIM
To state what the words "Jesus," "Christ," and "God with us" tell about God

QUICK READ
The eternal God of all that is took on human flesh in the person of Jesus of Nazareth in order that he might dwell with us and save us from our sins.

CHRISTMAS LESSON

Jesus—Christ—God with Us

On occasion I take myself much too seriously. As a pastor and writer, I am occupied with serious business, after all. I do my best to guide individuals through crises big and small. I research and formulate opinions about vexing theological conundrums. On a weekly basis I labor to creatively present the gospel and its implications for daily living, and I occasionally get the privilege of writing for BaptistWay Press. Imagine that!

Along with all of these responsibilities I am also a father. Although I am someone quite important with quite a lot to do (did I mention that I sometimes take myself too seriously), I try and take the time to let my children know that they are important to me and that I love them.

As of now, my youngest child is a slobbering, babbling, two-year-old little boy named Jack. Jack's favorite hobby is dirt. He sits in the dirt, he digs in the dirt, he throws the dirt up into the air, he puts the dirt into his pockets, and, yes, he sometimes likes to eat the dirt. One of the ways I try to let little Jack know how much I love him is to put all of my other important business on hold and kneel down to his level. I get down into the dirt. We're there together at eye level. We sit, we dig, and the dirt flies.

This is what Matthew was writing about in the beginning of his Gospel. If any being has the right to take himself seriously, it's God. The amazing thing is that this all-important, all-powerful God has taken the time to get down on our level, so to speak. As the Gospel of John says, "The Word became flesh and lived among us" (John 1:14). Or as Matthew says, "Emmanuel . . . God with us" (Matthew 1:23b). Father, Lord, Savior—down in the dirt with humanity; loving, rebuking, laughing, teaching, healing, saving, understanding. What does it all mean?

MATTHEW 1:18–25

18 Now the birth of Jesus the Messiah took place in this way. When his mother Mary had been engaged to Joseph, but before they lived together, she was found to be with child from the Holy Spirit. 19 Her husband Joseph, being a righteous man and unwilling to expose her to public disgrace, planned to dismiss her quietly. 20 But just when he had resolved to do this, an angel of the Lord

> appeared to him in a dream and said, "Joseph, son of David, do
> not be afraid to take Mary as your wife, for the child conceived in
> her is from the Holy Spirit. ²¹ She will bear a son, and you are to
> name him Jesus, for he will save his people from their sins." ²² All
> this took place to fulfill what had been spoken by the Lord through
> the prophet:
> ²³ "Look, the virgin shall conceive and bear a son,
> and they shall name him Emmanuel,"
> which means, "God is with us." ²⁴ When Joseph awoke from
> sleep, he did as the angel of the Lord commanded him; he took
> her as his wife, ²⁵ but had no marital relations with her until she
> had borne a son; and he named him Jesus.

A Child Conceived Out of Wedlock (1:18–19)

In one verse Matthew lets us know of the worrisome and scandalous predicament in which Mary found herself. Matthew also tells us about the nature of the relationship between Mary and Joseph. The New American Standard Bible reads that "Mary had been *betrothed* to Joseph" (1:18, italics added for emphasis). Trying to update this language a bit, the New Revised Standard Version says that "Mary had been *engaged* to Joseph" (italics added for emphasis). The New International Version says that "Mary was *pledged to be married* to Joseph" (italics added for emphasis).

Here's a way to understand this matter. Think of a situation in which parents arrange a marriage. Imagine that a father wants his son to marry a certain girl in town. The father of the girl agrees, and so the two are set to marry. The couple head down to the local courthouse with their fathers in tow, get a marriage license, and sign on the dotted line. Then they go their separate ways, and the girl continues living with her parents. The girl is now betrothed, that is, legally bound to the boy. About a year later, the couple has a wedding ceremony and consummate the marriage on their honeymoon. Now the girl has moved beyond betrothal to being fully a wife.

Therefore, although Mary was legally bound to Joseph, the two had not yet become one through sexual intercourse. Even so she was found

WHY DO THE GOSPELS DIFFER?

A number of detailed explanations can be given to explain and understand the differences that we find in the Gospel accounts. One important point to keep in mind is that we should take each Gospel on its own terms. Each Gospel was written to a unique set of circumstances, to specific people, and to address certain needs, with each human author desiring to emphasize different things.

A crucial extension of this point is that the Gospels are highly stylized documents. That is, each author constructed his individual Gospel in specific ways for specific reasons. A helpful analogy is to imagine (or watch) four different movies about some historical event such as the bombing of Pearl Harbor. Each film will contain the same factual elements but will differ in approach, style, overall theme, structure, dialogue, sub-plots, pace, etc. It doesn't mean that one film is right and the others are wrong. It means that each filmmaker is taking a different approach to telling the same story.

to be with child, the child who would come to be known as Jesus Christ. The term *Christ* is not a name but a title. It is the Greek rendering of the Hebrew word *Messiah*, which means *anointed*. In Old Testament times certain people, especially kings, were anointed with oil to signify that they had a unique relationship with God. When the title *Christ* was used with the name *Jesus*, people meant something like this: *Jesus, God's anointed*, or even *King Jesus*.

So Mary's child was from God. However, this was surely not the main reason for the whispering that was occurring all over town. Joseph and Mary had not come together, and Mary was pregnant. Scandalous indeed.

Verse 19 tells us a great deal about Joseph's character and his love for Mary. After finding out that Mary had seemingly been unfaithful to him, he certainly knew what his rights were as a Jewish male. Thus he planned to divorce her but to "dismiss her quietly" (Matt. 1:19), privately. He had no desire to make a public spectacle of her. This decision speaks volumes about his character, revealing that he was a caring, gentle, and merciful soul.

A Child Conceived by the Holy Spirit (1:20–25)

Just when Joseph laid his plans and resolved to follow through with them, God unveiled his larger plan. Through an angel God told Joseph not to be afraid to take Mary as his wife and that the child conceived in her was from the Holy Spirit. Mary had not been unfaithful at all. Rather, God had chosen her to carry God's only begotten Son, who was to be named Jesus, "for he will save his people from their sins" (1:21). The name of this child is directly linked to what his mission would be. The name *Jesus* is the Greek form of the Hebrew name *Joshua*. Joshua means, *Yahweh saves*. Thus, this one called Jesus would be the agent through whom God would save his people.

Matthew indicates that this in fact was nothing new, but that it had actually been God's plan for some time. All of these events were happening to fulfill what was spoken through the prophet Isaiah, who said, "Look, the virgin shall conceive and bear a son and they shall name him Emmanuel" (1:23; Isaiah 7:14). While Isaiah originally spoke these words to King Ahaz to assure him that his enemies in the Syro-Ephraimite War would not defeat him, the fuller meaning of this text pointed to a much greater deliverance. The promise was not merely an assurance against earthly enemies or worldly armies but against the unseen powers of evil, against the spiritual forces that hold us captive to sin and rebellion.

But how is this assurance of safety and deliverance to the human race finally worked out? Just how are the evil forces that hold creation captive overthrown? This is the part that, if we're not thoughtful enough, we can either take for granted because we've heard it so many times or fail to appreciate just how surprising it all is because such a radical idea has grown stale with time. What is God's answer to the violence that Satan has worked against his plan and to every form of idolatry and rebellion on the part of humankind? A baby.

That is just the beginning of it, of course. Although many would like to keep Jesus tiny and unthreatening, we must be careful and not forever restrict him to the manger. The baby grew up to become a man who taught about something called the kingdom of God and healed people of all sorts of ailments. These incredible things didn't last long, however. He was sentenced to death and executed. According to the eyewitness testimony of the earliest disciples, he was raised from the dead, and afterward he ascended into heaven.

So how is all of that a solution to the powers of evil and rebellion? The astonishing answer to that question is that Jesus brought death to those things—by bringing death to himself. Jesus punished evil by taking the punishment on himself.

This child that Mary carried would eventually heal all of humanity by taking on our infirmities, our diseases, our guilt as his own (Isa. 53:4–5). The sin of humanity is blotted out because of one man's righteousness. The rebellion of a whole race is made right through one man's obedience. As Paul succinctly puts it in 2 Corinthians 5:21: "For our sake he made him to be sin who knew no sin, so that in him we might become the righteousness of God."

Now all of that sounds like a really bad deal for Jesus, and it was. However, without trivializing his agony and death on the cross in any way, we can safely say that it's not as bad as it sounds. Because he was so righteous, because he lived a life of sinless perfection, death could not hold him. Agony and death were not the end of the story. He laid his life down in obedience to God only to take it back up again—his life and ours!

Moreover, when we take a closer look at this man named Jesus, we discover that he actually isn't just *any* man. He is the preexistent, eternal Word (John 1:1). He is God's "only Son" (John 3:16). He is one with the

WHAT IS THE CELEBRATION OF CHRISTMAS REALLY ALL ABOUT?

- God loves humanity so much that he decided to take human form.
- We are not without hope because Jesus Christ acts as Mediator between God and humanity.
- The good news of Christmas is that "in Christ God was reconciling the world to himself, not counting their trespasses against them, and entrusting the message of reconciliation to us" (2 Cor. 5:19). Let us not forget what Paul said at the end of verse 19. This message of reconciliation has been committed to the church.

Father (John 10:30). He is "the image of the invisible God" (Colossians 1:15). He is God in the flesh, God with us. Emmanuel.

The God of all that is, stooped down to us here on planet Earth in all of our slobbering and babbling and dug around in the dirt with us. That's how God demonstrates his love for us. Now that's worthy of a hearty Merry Christmas!

Implications and Actions

So we're back to the question, *What does it all mean?* Put simply it means that Christmas is about God breaking into our world. He didn't break in on us seeking to strong arm us into his way of doing things. He came gently, unassumingly. The eternal God clothed himself with human flesh and told us about his love for us in a way that we could understand. He would eventually demonstrate that love by taking the grisly consequences of sin upon himself.

Before we were able to tiptoe one centimeter in God's direction, he spanned the entire chasm in one step. It's our move.

QUESTIONS

1. Why do you think the idea of God taking on human flesh is difficult for some people to believe?

2. What are some of the implications of God breaking into and acting in the course of human history?

3. What does the name *Jesus* tell us about the character of God?

4. Can you define the following terms: Jesus, Christ, Emmanuel?

Our Next New Study

(Available for use beginning March 2013)

PSALMS:
Songs from the Heart of Faith

How to Order More Bible Study Materials

It's easy! Just fill in the following information. For additional Bible study materials available both in print and online, see www.baptistwaypress.org, or get a complete order form of available print materials—including Spanish materials—by calling 1-866-249-1799 or e-mailing baptistway@texasbaptists.org.

Title of item	Price	Quantity	Cost
This Issue:			
The Gospel of Mark: People Responding to Jesus—Study Guide (BWP001147)	$3.95	_____	_____
The Gospel of Mark: People Responding to Jesus—Large Print Study Guide (BWP001148)	$4.25	_____	_____
The Gospel of Mark: People Responding to Jesus—Teaching Guide (BWP001149)	$4.95	_____	_____
Additional Issues Available:			
Growing Together in Christ—Study Guide (BWP001036)	$3.25	_____	_____
Growing Together in Christ—Teaching Guide (BWP001038)	$3.75	_____	_____
Living Generously for Jesus' Sake—Study Guide (BWP001137)	$3.95	_____	_____
Living Generously for Jesus' Sake—Large Print Study Guide (BWP001138)	$4.25	_____	_____
Living Generously for Jesus' Sake—Teaching Guide (BWP001139)	$4.95	_____	_____
Living Faith in Daily Life—Study Guide (BWP001095)	$3.55	_____	_____
Living Faith in Daily Life—Large Print Study Guide (BWP001096)	$3.95	_____	_____
Living Faith in Daily Life—Teaching Guide (BWP001097)	$4.25	_____	_____
Participating in God's Mission—Study Guide (BWP001077)	$3.55	_____	_____
Participating in God's Mission—Large Print Study Guide (BWP001078)	$3.95	_____	_____
Participating in God's Mission—Teaching Guide (BWP001079)	$3.95	_____	_____
Profiles in Character—Study Guide (BWP001112)	$3.55	_____	_____
Profiles in Character—Large Print Study Guide (BWP001113)	$4.25	_____	_____
Profiles in Character—Teaching Guide (BWP001114)	$4.95	_____	_____
Genesis: People Relating to God—Study Guide (BWP001088)	$2.35	_____	_____
Genesis: People Relating to God—Large Print Study Guide (BWP001089)	$2.75	_____	_____
Genesis: People Relating to God—Teaching Guide (BWP001090)	$2.95	_____	_____
Genesis 12—50: Family Matters—Study Guide (BWP000034)	$1.95	_____	_____
Genesis 12—50: Family Matters—Teaching Guide (BWP000035)	$2.45	_____	_____
Leviticus, Numbers, Deuteronomy—Study Guide (BWP000053)	$2.35	_____	_____
Leviticus, Numbers, Deuteronomy—Large Print Study Guide (BWP000052)	$2.35	_____	_____
Leviticus, Numbers, Deuteronomy—Teaching Guide (BWP000054)	$2.95	_____	_____
1 and 2 Kings: Leaders and Followers—Study Guide (BWP001025)	$2.95	_____	_____
1 and 2 Kings: Leaders and Followers—Large Print Study Guide (BWP001026)	$3.15	_____	_____
1 and 2 Kings: Leaders and Followers—Teaching Guide (BWP001027)	$3.45	_____	_____
Ezra, Haggai, Zechariah, Nehemiah, Malachi—Study Guide (BWP001071)	$3.25	_____	_____
Ezra, Haggai, Zechariah, Nehemiah, Malachi—Large Print Study Guide (BWP001072)	$3.55	_____	_____
Ezra, Haggai, Zechariah, Nehemiah, Malachi—Teaching Guide (BWP001073)	$3.75	_____	_____
Job, Ecclesiastes, Habakkuk, Lamentations—Study Guide (BWP001016)	$2.75	_____	_____
Job, Ecclesiastes, Habakkuk, Lamentations—Large Print Study Guide (BWP001017)	$2.85	_____	_____
Job, Ecclesiastes, Habakkuk, Lamentations—Teaching Guide (BWP001018)	$3.25	_____	_____
Psalms and Proverbs—Study Guide (BWP001000)	$2.75	_____	_____
Psalms and Proverbs—Teaching Guide (BWP001002)	$3.25	_____	_____
Amos. Hosea, Isaiah, Micah: Calling for Justice, Mercy, and Faithfulness—Study Guide (BWP001132)	$3.95	_____	_____
Amos. Hosea, Isaiah, Micah: Calling for Justice, Mercy, and Faithfulness—Large Print Study Guide (BWP001133)	$4.25	_____	_____
Amos. Hosea, Isaiah, Micah: Calling for Justice, Mercy, and Faithfulness—Teaching Guide (BWP001134)	$4.95	_____	_____
The Gospel of Matthew: A Primer for Discipleship—Study Guide (BWP001127)	$3.95	_____	_____
The Gospel of Matthew: A Primer for Discipleship—Large Print Study Guide (BWP001128)	$4.25	_____	_____
The Gospel of Matthew: A Primer for Discipleship—Teaching Guide (BWP001129)	$4.95	_____	_____
Matthew: Hope in the Resurrected Christ—Study Guide (BWP001066)	$3.25	_____	_____
Matthew: Hope in the Resurrected Christ—Large Print Study Guide (BWP001067)	$3.55	_____	_____
Matthew: Hope in the Resurrected Christ—Teaching Guide (BWP001068)	$3.75	_____	_____
Mark: Jesus' Works and Words—Study Guide (BWP001022)	$2.95	_____	_____
Mark: Jesus' Works and Words—Large Print Study Guide (BWP001023)	$3.15	_____	_____
Mark:Jesus' Works and Words—Teaching Guide (BWP001024)	$3.45	_____	_____
Jesus in the Gospel of Mark—Study Guide (BWP000066)	$1.95	_____	_____
Jesus in the Gospel of Mark—Teaching Guide (BWP000067)	$2.45	_____	_____
Luke: Journeying to the Cross—Study Guide (BWP000057)	$2.35	_____	_____
Luke: Journeying to the Cross—Large Print Study Guide (BWP000056)	$2.35	_____	_____
Luke: Journeying to the Cross—Teaching Guide (BWP000058)	$2.95	_____	_____
The Gospel of John: Light Overcoming Darkness, Part One—Study Guide (BWP001104)	$3.55	_____	_____
The Gospel of John: Light Overcoming Darkness, Part One—Large Print Study Guide (BWP001105)	$3.95	_____	_____
The Gospel of John: Light Overcoming Darkness, Part One—Teaching Guide (BWP001106)	$4.50	_____	_____
The Gospel of John: Light Overcoming Darkness, Part Two—Study Guide (BWP001109)	$3.55	_____	_____
The Gospel of John: Light Overcoming Darkness, Part Two—Large Print Study Guide (BWP001110)	$3.95	_____	_____
The Gospel of John: Light Overcoming Darkness, Part Two—Teaching Guide (BWP001111)	$4.50	_____	_____
The Gospel of John: The Word Became Flesh—Study Guide (BWP001008)	$2.75	_____	_____
The Gospel of John: The Word Became Flesh—Large Print Study Guide (BWP001009)	$2.85	_____	_____
The Gospel of John: The Word Became Flesh—Teaching Guide (BWP001010)	$3.25	_____	_____
The Book of Acts: Time to Act on Acts 1:8—Study Guide (BWP001142)	$3.95	_____	_____
The Book of Acts: Time to Act on Acts 1:8—Large Print Study Guide (BWP001143)	$4.25	_____	_____
The Book of Acts: Time to Act on Acts 1:8—Teaching Guide (BWP001144)	$4.95	_____	_____

Item	Price		
Acts: Toward Being a Missional Church—Study Guide (BWP001013)	$2.75	_____	_____
Acts: Toward Being a Missional Church—Large Print Study Guide (BWP001014)	$2.85	_____	_____
Acts: Toward Being a Missional Church—Teaching Guide (BWP001015)	$3.25	_____	_____
Romans: What God Is Up To—Study Guide (BWP001019)	$2.95	_____	_____
Romans: What God Is Up To—Large Print Study Guide (BWP001020)	$3.15	_____	_____
Romans: What God Is Up To—Teaching Guide (BWP001021)	$3.45	_____	_____
The Corinthian Letters—Study Guide (BWP001121)	$3.55	_____	_____
The Corinthian Letters—Large Print Study Guide (BWP001122)	$4.25	_____	_____
The Corinthian Letters—Teaching Guide (BWP001123)	$4.95	_____	_____
Galatians and 1&2 Thessalonians—Study Guide (BWP001080)	$3.55	_____	_____
Galatians and 1&2 Thessalonians—Large Print Study Guide (BWP001081)	$3.95	_____	_____
Galatians and 1&2 Thessalonians—Teaching Guide (BWP001082)	$3.95	_____	_____
1, 2 Timothy, Titus, Philemon—Study Guide (BWP000092)	$2.75	_____	_____
1, 2 Timothy, Titus, Philemon—Teaching Guide (BWP000093)	$3.25	_____	_____
Letters of James and John—Study Guide (BWP001101)	$3.55	_____	_____
Letters of James and John—Large Print Study Guide (BWP001102)	$3.95	_____	_____
Letters of James and John—Teaching Guide (BWP001103)	$4.25	_____	_____

Coming for use beginning March 2013

Item	Price		
Psalms: Songs from the Heart of Faith—Study Guide (BWP001152)	$3.95	_____	_____
Psalms: Songs from the Heart of Faith—Large Print Study Guide (BWP001153)	$4.25	_____	_____
Psalms: Songs from the Heart of Faith—Teaching Guide (BWP001154)	$4.95	_____	_____

Standard (UPS/Mail) Shipping Charges*			
Order Value	Shipping charge**	Order Value	Shipping charge**
$.01—$9.99	$6.50	$160.00—$199.99	$24.00
$10.00—$19.99	$8.50	$200.00—$249.99	$28.00
$20.00—$39.99	$9.50	$250.00—$299.99	$30.00
$40.00—$59.99	$10.50	$300.00—$349.99	$34.00
$60.00—$79.99	$11.50	$350.00—$399.99	$42.00
$80.00—$99.99	$12.50	$400.00—$499.99	$50.00
$100.00—$129.99	$15.00	$500.00—$599.99	$60.00
$130.00—$159.99	$20.00	$600.00—$799.99	$72.00**

Cost of items (Order value) _____

Shipping charges (see chart*) _____

TOTAL _____

*Plus, applicable taxes for individuals and other taxable entities (not churches) within Texas will be added. Please call 1-866-249-1799 if the exact amount is needed prior to ordering.

**For order values $800.00 and above, please call 1-866-249-1799 or check www.baptistwaypress.org

Please allow three weeks for standard delivery. For express shipping service: Call 1-866-249-1799 for information on additional charges.

YOUR NAME _____ PHONE _____

YOUR CHURCH _____ DATE ORDERED _____

SHIPPING ADDRESS _____

CITY _____ STATE _____ ZIP CODE _____

E-MAIL _____

MAIL this form with your check for the total amount to
BAPTISTWAY PRESS, Baptist General Convention of Texas,
333 North Washington, Dallas, TX 75246-1798
(Make checks to "Baptist Executive Board.")

OR, **FAX** your order anytime to: 214-828-5376, and we will bill you.

OR, **CALL** your order toll-free: 1-866-249-1799
(M-Fri 8:30 a.m.-5:00 p.m. central time), and we will bill you.

OR, **E-MAIL** your order to our internet e-mail address:
baptistway@texasbaptists.org, and we will bill you.

OR, **ORDER ONLINE** at www.baptistwaypress.org.

We look forward to receiving your order! Thank you!